WADSWORTH PHILOSOPHERS SERIES

ON

JUNG

Richard Bilsker
College of Southern Maryland

D1522543

WADSWORTH

★ ™

THOMSON LEARNING

Australia • Canada • Mexico • Singapore • Spain
United Kingdom • United States

Printed in the United States of America
1 2 3 4 5 6 7 04 03 02 01 00

For permission to use material from this text, contact us:
Web: http://www.thomsonrights.com
Fax: 1-800-730-2215
Phone: 1-800-730-2214

For more information, contact:
Wadsworth/Thomson Learning, Inc.
10 Davis Drive
Belmont, CA 94002-3098
USA
http://www.wadsworth.com

ISBN: 0-534-58378-4

Contents

Preface

In the 1950s, Carl Gustav Jung was still considered by many to be a renegade Freudian. Even though Jung was invited independently of Freud in 1909 to visit Clark University, Jung was not embraced as easily by American psychiatrists and psychologists. Today, however, is a different story. In most American bookstores you will find many more books written by Jung, about Jung, or influenced by Jung than you will for Freud. Freud has a more lasting presence in introductory psychology textbooks, and perhaps Freudian terminology has become more prevalent in common speech, but Jung's ideas are in some ways more resonant at this turn of the century. Many people are aware of personality tests in magazines and workplaces. In a major way these can be traced back to Jung's categorizations of psychological types. Through the popular books, lectures, and television work of his follower Joseph Campbell, many people have become aware of Jung's views on the common sources of all world mythologies and religions.

In one major way this is puzzling: Jung is much more difficult to read than Freud is. In most cases, you can pick up one of Freud's books and immediately figure out where he is headed. His works generally begin with a history of his subject and an explanation of where he views his own position with regard to this history. Jung's style is not as self-contained. Jung presupposes much more of his readers than does Freud. He also explores material that is quite esoteric. Freud refers to works of philosophers, earlier psychologists, anthropologists, and literary works. Jung refers to all of these, as well. Jung, though, also explores world religions and mythologies in great detail. He also looks at the alchemical tradition in much of his later work. Most people view the alchemists as proto-chemists; Jung reads them as proto-psychologists. In addition, Jung seems to have a difficulty in expressing himself in clearly understandable language. The thread of his argument is frequently interrupted by new topics that delay the return to the main argument.

So, authors of books like the one you hold in your hands face a challenge: how do you present Jung's ideas in a readable format without sacrificing something that Jung himself considers quite important? As this book is part of a series of books on philosophers, I have concentrated my efforts on presenting Jung's view of human nature as his most central philosophical concern. This does not limit my discussion as much as one might think. For this reason, though, I do not discuss his many writings on the practice of psychotherapy, except when the therapy is used as an example (or offered as proof) of his theoretical views. This topic is dealt with more than adequately in books about Jungian therapy.

Many books on Jung end up as no more than a comparison with Freud. It is easy to see why, as Freud is easily the most visible figure in twentieth century psychology and Jung was professionally associated with Freud or his work for nearly a decade. I mention Freud as little as possible in order to let Jung's ideas stand for themselves. This has been easier to do in some places than in others (as this preface itself indicates!).

There is a limitation, however, that most introductory books on Jung make that I have not. Of the introductory books on Jung listed in the bibliography, almost all ignore the alchemical and mythological studies Jung made in the last twenty-five years of his life. Part of this is because of the difficulty in understanding why Jung discusses these topics and part of it is that the books are meant as summaries of Jung's views on psychology and many authors do not consider these later writings to be about psychology. Jung, on the other hand, considered these later writings to be his most important. So, the longest chapter of this book considers these difficult topics in such a way that the reader should come away with a sense of what Jung's ideas and goals were.

This book is different from other introductory books in another way. Jung mentions philosophers in most of his works, including his dissertation. There is only one work that is explicitly about philosophy and that is his lecture series on Nietzsche's book *Thus Spake Zarathustra*. Jung's lectures, published in 1988 (and in an abridged form in 1998), are considered here as they provide another way into understanding his view of human nature.

A third difference between the book in your hands and other accounts of Jung's ideas is that I will point the reader to subjects other than psychology. Where appropriate you will also find references to works on history, science, religion, and anthropology, as well as literature.

Chapter 1 of this book is a sketch of Jung's life. From there, Jung's psychoanalytic writings are considered in Chapter 2. Chapter 3 is a presentation of the major ideas developed by Jung in his immediately post-Freudian period. Jung's lectures from 1934-1939 on Nietzsche's *Zarathustra* are the subject of Chapter 4. Chapter 5 addresses Jung's later writings on religion, alchemy, and mythology. Throughout all of these chapters you will find that references to Jung's *Collected Works* contain the abbreviation *CW* along with a volume number, for ease of reference.

Jung is a fascinating figure. I first encountered him, along with Freud, in my first-year English composition course in college. We were asked to work on our writing skills by responding to writings in the history of ideas. I have read and taught Freud and Jung many times since then and always find something of interest. It is my hope that what you read here will stimulate you to continue your explorations of Jung and the history of ideas, as well.

I would like to thank all the family, friends, teachers, students, and colleagues who have broadened my mind and engaged me in the great conversation, provided me with support and understanding, and helped me grow as a person.

1
Jung's Life

Jung's Early Life

Carl Gustav Jung was born in Kesswil, Switzerland on July 26, 1875. His father, Johann Paul Jung, was a pastor in the Swiss church. Jung's mother, Emilie Jung-Preiswerk, was the daughter of a minister. Although Jung would himself be intimately concerned with religious ideas throughout his life, he would ultimately reject the type of Christianity practiced by his father. The family moved to the parsonage of Laufen Castle when Jung was a few months old. The relationship between his parents was often strained and his mother spent some time in a sanitarium.

Jung's Education

Jung went away to the Basel Gymnasium, a boarding school, when he was eleven. Jung attended the University of Basel and ultimately completed a medical degree. His interests were initially split between the humanities (history and philosophy) and the sciences (natural science and archaeology). As his family was living on a modest parson's income he decided against a career in the humanities which gave fewer opportunities for employment. He was leaning toward archaeology, but Basel had no faculty in the subject, and the monetary concerns precluded going elsewhere. Eventually, Jung's studies, as we shall see, lead him to perform what could be called an archaeology of the mind. So, Jung decided on medicine since it would both allow him to study the sciences and provide an income after graduation. Jung did not immediately choose the specialization in psychiatry, though. His decision only came after much thought. In fact, psychiatry was a subject he delayed in studying for as long as he could. When he finally started to read a textbook on psychiatry by Krafft-Ebing, he knew this was the field he should enter. It was Krafft-Ebing's unassuming honesty and lack of pretense about shortcomings in the scientific foundations of psychiatry that had won Jung over to psychiatry. Jung's dissertation, *On the Psychology and Pathology of so-called Occult Phenomena*, which was published later in 1902, introduced his interest in paranormal studies.[1] This interest would underlie much of what follows in the development of his career path.

Jung's Professional Life

Jung had a long and prolific career from his first appointment at Burghölzli through his lectureship in Zurich and his tremendously successful private practice. He continued teaching and writing in one form or another throughout his long life.

Burghölzli and Psychoanalysis

In 1900, Jung accepted an appointment as an assistant at the Burghölzli Mental Hospital in Zurich. At the hospital, because of his work with patients, Jung started to develop ideas about the causes of psychosis and forms of therapy that would lead to an association with Freud's Psychoanalysis. He became acquainted with Freud's work while at the hospital; he saw connections with his own work. The two formally met in 1907 and their professional relationship lasted until 1913. This period of intellectual development is the subject for the next chapter. His appointment at Burghölzli also meant that Jung could afford to marry Emma Rauschenbach in 1903. In 1905, he became lecturer in psychiatry at the University of Zurich and was promoted to senior physician at the hospital. Jung traveled to the United States with Freud (who was invited independently) in 1909, where they lectured at Clark University in Worcester, Massachusetts. While in Massachusetts he befriended William James. James, who died the following year, taught Philosophy, Physiology, and Psychology at Harvard and was a leading figure in the Pragmatist movement.[2] Jung resigned his post at the hospital in 1909 to concentrate on his rapidly expanding private practice.

"The Night Journey of the Soul"

After publishing *Transformation and Symbols of the Libido*, the book that marked the end of the relationship with Freud, Jung entered a period of more than three years in which he did not do much writing and was quite reclusive. Depending on whose version of these events you believe, he either suffered a complete mental breakdown or he was merely exploring his own unconscious. It is clear that this self-reflective period began in 1913. It is not clear, however, whether it lasted until 1917, 1918, or 1919.[3] During this period he resigned his teaching position, drastically reduced the number of patients he saw, and resigned from the chairmanship of the International Psychoanalytic Association (a position Freud strongly urged him to accept). This is also the time period in which Jung, through his study of Gnosticism (an early Christian heresy), Alchemy (an ancient and medieval spiritual forerunner of chemistry and psychology), and Asian thought (particularly Indian and Chinese philosophy), began to develop his unique views on human nature and psychotherapy.

The Emergence of Analytical Psychology

Jung fully emerged from the self-reflective period with the publication of the first of his major works, *Psychological Types*, in 1921. In this book, Jung provides a way of categorizing and understanding different personality types. Between this book and the publication of his last major work before World War II, the Terry Lectures at Yale, *Psychology and Religion*, Jung wrote and published the more than sixty books, articles, and lectures that he is most identified with and define his basic views. The views that are developed in these major works will be discussed in Chapter 3.

The Second World War

Jung continued to write and work during World War II, though he did not publish at quite the pace that he did in the previous fifteen years. During the war, his researches into Gnosticism and alchemy continued, as did his interest in Asian philosophy. As with discussion of his time after the split with Freud, there is controversy over Jung's views on Jews and Hitler during the war. Portrayals of Jung vary from considering him ambivalent to Nazism and Anti-Semitism to him being rabidly Nazi. Like so much of Jung's views, his thought here is very complicated.[4] Jung's health also became a concern during this period. He suffered a heart attack and had a prolonged hospital stay during 1944. He did not think he would survive. By war's end, Jung was seventy years old and recovering his health.

Jung's Later Years

In order to recover his health more completely, Jung officially retired after the war. Most of the works published between 1948 and 1961, the year he died, are either reworkings and expansions of his earlier writings, or were concerned with issues raised by his researches into religion, Asian thought, and the paranormal (a topic that had interested him throughout his career). The writings of this period are considered in Chapter 5. In 1958, after much prodding by his students and associates, Jung began work, with Aniela Jaffé, on his autobiography, which was published after his death as *Memories, Dreams, Reflections*. During this period Jung received many awards and honorary degrees, and was greatly appreciated around the world. His wife Emma died in 1955, and Carl Gustav Jung died June 6, 1961.

Notes

[1] "On the Psychology and Pathology of so-called Occult Phenomena," in *CW*, vol. 1., pp. 3-88.

[2] For more on this visit, see the Rosenzweig book listed in bibliography.

[3] I cannot settle the matter here. The interested reader should consult Jung's own account in *Memories, Dreams, Reflections*, and the works in the biography section of the bibliography.

[4] Here, too, the interested reader must consult the differing accounts in the bibliography.

2

The Psychoanalytic Years

Introduction

It is often thought that Jung did not begin making contributions to psychology until after he had met Freud. Jung had already started working at Burghölzli before he became interested in Freud. Jung had been dealing with patients at the clinic and was becoming aware of the relevance of Freud in a gradual way. It is not until his 1906 book on schizophrenia, *The Psychology of Dementia Praecox*, that he contacted Freud and they begin their brief but important working relationship.[1]

This chapter's concern is Jung's early work, from his doctoral dissertation, "On the Psychology and Pathology of So-called Occult Phenomena," to *Symbols of Transformation*, the work that precipitated the break with Freud.[2] Because of the importance of Freud's development of psychoanalysis, Freud is discussed more in this chapter than in the others.

Another aspect of both Freud and Jung that is not always made clear by treatments of their work is that they both had extensive scientific training. As was mentioned last chapter, Jung chose to be a medical doctor for financial reasons and a psychiatrist because of the Krafft-Ebing textbook. Jung, while at Burghölzli, was engaged in research on the brain tissue of deceased schizophrenics. The prevailing view was that there must be *something* wrong with their brains. Jung, like others, could not find what that something was. Although he kept up with the research of others when it was published, he became more interested in the psychological aspects of schizophrenia. Much more is known about the physiological and genetic bases of schizophrenia today, but it is still not a mystery solved. Freud was a neurologist at first, and he became a therapist from financial and political concerns. Freud was aware that he would not be able to secure a teaching appointment in Vienna due to anti-Semitism. Like Jung, Freud's background as a medical doctor had started with the physiological basis of mental phenomena. Freud was intrigued by the recent discovery of the existence of neurons. He began work on a book he was calling *Project for a Scientific Psychology*. In this book, eventually published posthumously in 1950, Freud wanted to tie mental functioning to the physiological. As the science of the time was not sophisticated enough, the *Project* was in some sense doomed from the start. So, as Jung did after him, Freud focused primarily on the psychological for the rest of his career. Another similarity in the early Freud and early Jung is that both, early in their careers, had connections to the work of the French psychologist Jean Martin Charcot (1825-1893). Freud worked directly with Charcot in 1885-1886, and in 1902, Jung worked with Charcot's student, the French psychiatrist Pierre Janet (1859-1947). Charcot and Janet were both concerned with hysteria and hypnosis.[3]

The Dissertation

Many of the ideas that Jung would develop more fully later in his career are already found in his dissertation, "On the Psychology and Pathology of So-called Occult Phenomena." The dissertation is primarily an analysis of S.W., "A Case of Somnambulism in a Girl with Poor Inheritance." She was a young girl who was "channeling" (to use the more modern term) the spirit of her dead grandfather, who spoke of Jung's grandfather and others during trance-like states. Jung observed these states and "table-turning" events (similar to Ouija board experiences). Many years later, we find out that S.W. was Jung's cousin. This is the reason that Jung was able to attend the table-turning sessions and explains S.W.'s mentioning of Jung's grandfather. As this was his dissertation, Jung is very modest in his analysis. He surveys the existing literature and draws several humble conclusions. Jung recognizes that many of the similar cases reported involve people going through puberty. He postulates that the forming of one's personality for adulthood can be a cause: "we must suppose that there was some connection between these disturbances and the physiological changes of character at puberty."[4] Drawing on Freud's work in *The Interpretation of Dreams* and *Studies on Hysteria*, Jung concludes that the strong, older woman personality that S.W. calls Ivenes, is a kind of wish-fulfilment. That is, it is "the woman's premonition of sexual feeling.... nothing but a dream of sexual wish-fulfilment."[5] Although Freud is mentioned in only three places in the dissertation, Jung admits his importance in his response to a critical review of his book. In his reply to the critic Hahn, Jung says that his "analysis of the clinical picture is not, as Mr. Hahn thinks, based on the French writers, but on Freud's investigations of hysteria."[6]

It should also be noted that Jung was also careful, at the beginning of the discussion of S.W., to mention her family history (note the phrase "poor inheritance" in the title of the section of his dissertation concerned with S.W.). He lists her relatives with mental problems: her paternal grandfather had "waking hallucinations," one of her grandfather's brothers was "feeble-minded, an eccentric," the paternal grandmother had a three-day trance after a case of what might have been typhoid and often "uttered prophecies," her father and two brothers of his were odd, with "bizarre ideas," and a third brother of her father was "eccentric and odd, talented but one-sided," and S.W.'s mother had "a congenital psychopathic inferiority often bordering on psychosis," a sister of S.W. was "an hysteric and a visionary," and finally, one of her other sisters "suffers from 'nervous heart attacks.'" As mentioned in the introduction to this chapter, Jung was more concerned with the possibility of physical causes in his early work.[7]

Before the analysis of S.W., Jung discusses the case of Miss E. Miss E. claimed to see dead people during what she called "attacks of delirium." She did not remember these events when she returned to her "fully conscious" states. S.W. also had this memory loss when shifting states. S.W., however, seems to move beyond the strange experiences as she gets older. Miss E., already an adult of 40, slips into the delirium during times of stress. At the end of the work Jung says he mentioned Miss E. in the beginning of the book in order to compare pathological and non-pathological versions of somnambulism. He is using the word "somnambulism" here in a sense that is broader than the English equivalent, "sleepwalking." In the dissertation, all forms of seemingly conscious behavior that are not remembered by the primary, or dominant, personality will be considered somnambulistic.[8]

As we will soon see, some other themes that are introduced here will be discussed in later chapters. Briefly, let me mention them. Later, Jung will take occult phenomena even more seriously, placing some of the causal elements outside of the individual's own experiences. Here, as we saw, he seeks an explanation in S.W.'s and Miss E.'s actual lives. Chapter 3 will consider Jung's full development of the concept of the impersonal, or "collective," unconscious. Later in this chapter we will consider the first hints of this in *Symbols of Transformation*. Jung also quotes Friedrich Nietzsche's *Thus Spake Zarathustra* in the dissertation. Jung does not analyze the text he quotes, though. He only mentions it as an example of cryptomnesia. That is, a case in which one says something that one thinks originates in oneself, when it is actually something you came into contact with before, but you no longer remember the experience. Jung's analysis of Nietzsche's *Zarathustra* will be discussed in Chapter 4.

The Association Tests

While at Burghölzli, Jung also initiated what came to be called association tests.[9] These were not unlike what Freud independently called free association. Jung, however, unlike Freud, studied word association in an experimental setting. Jung would ask a subject to respond to a word with the first word that came to mind. The subject was timed regarding the interval between the stimulus (the word spoken by Jung) and the response (the subject's word) for about a hundred words. Jung discovered that the subject took more time to respond to words in areas that the subject had some level of emotional significance. In most cases, the subject was unaware of the delay in reaction time. In paying attention to reaction times, the observer/analyst can determine problem areas, areas that might surround some Freudian repression. These are areas in which energy is spent to keep the idea(s) unconscious.

Another thing Jung noticed in his studies is that often people intimately connected with each other, for example, parents and children, or spouses, would pause over the same stimulus words! This, Jung thought, would be problematic as it could inhibit people from developing as strong individuals. It might even adversely affect the analyst. From his association tests, Jung developed his theory of the complexes, which is the next major idea found in his early work.

The Complexes

A complex is a collection of associations. For Jung, the concept of the complexes was important for a number of reasons. For one, the evidence of unconscious complexes would seem to bear out the Freudian theory of repression. Also, it provided further evidence for Jung's view that the mind could be viewed as containing partial personalities.[10]

These complexes are autonomous: they tend to act on their own, having physical, as well as psychical effects. They can affect the stomach, heart, and/or lungs, for example. In his 1935 Lectures, Jung says of them that our personalities consist of an "indefinite, because unknown, number of complexes or fragmentary personalities."[11]

It was his view of complexes as partial personalities that led Jung to try to understand the psychological aspects of schizophrenia. The work on schizophrenia, which ultimately led to the personal relationship with Freud, is the topic of the next section.

Psychoanalysis and Schizophrenia

Prior to the work that led to his book, *The Psychology of Dementia Praecox*, it was thought that schizophrenia (then called *dementia praecox*), was to be understood as purely organic. By learning the life stories of the patients at Burghölzli, Jung was able to notice certain links between the earlier lives of the patients and their current behaviors. In one example, a woman who had been in the hospital for fifty years repeatedly made motions resembling a village cobbler. After her death, Jung found out that right before her madness she had been rejected by a shoemaker she had been in love with. In other cases, Jung noticed that the fantasies of psychotic patients could be understood in the same way as dreams if using Freudian techniques of dream analysis. Eventually, Jung determined that psychoses were not as amenable to Freudian treatment as were the neuroses that Freud usually dealt with. Even as late as 1958, Jung was not sure what the balance was between the organic and the psychological in the development of schizophrenia.[12] The idea that not everything could be traced to sexual trauma would soon end the brief personal relationship with Freud that the book on schizophrenia initiated.

Transformational Symbols

In 1912, Jung published the book that has become known as *Symbols of Transformation*. The book, when first published, had the title *Transformations and Symbols of the Libido*. To make things more confusing, in 1916 the first translation of the book into English was titled *Psychology of the Unconscious*. Volume 5 of Jung's Collected Works, *Symbols of Transformation: An Analysis of the Prelude to a Case of Schizophrenia* contains the fourth edition of the book. In 1992, Princeton University Press republished the original 1916 translation as a supplement to the *Collected Works*. Why does this book merit so much editorializing?

Symbols of Transformation is the book of Jung's that firmly established him as an independent thinker. It clearly drew the boundaries between his views and Freud's published views. Freud took the book to be a personal attack and betrayal. Although in some way the book, like the book discussed in the preceding section, is about schizophrenia, Jung was moving more toward the psychological and farther away from the medical perspective of his dissertation.

The Revision and the Original

There is a further reason for editorializing. In the *Standard Edition* of Freud's works, great care is taken by the editors to make it clear what was added and/or deleted from each work as it was reprinted in new editions. Jung, however, did not revisit older works nearly as frequently as Freud did. Jung was much more likely to write a new work and then footnote his other writings as a signal of expansion, or alteration of previous paths. *Symbols of Transformation* is different. In 1950, Jung decided for the work's fourth edition, to significantly revise the book. The editors of the *Collected Works*, however, did not point out those changes, nor did Jung in most cases. If you are not familiar with the original version, you cannot tell whether what you are reading should be read as the insight of 1912 or the hindsight of 1950. Reading only the later version will prevent us from gaining a picture of the nature of the break with Freud at the time it was happening.[13] Before considering the text itself the question of why Jung revised the book at all needs to be addressed.

In the "Foreword to the Fourth (Swiss) Edition," Jung tells us what prompted him to return to this book after "thirty-seven years." The primary reason he gives, speaking in a personal manner, is

> I have never felt happy about this book, much less satisfied with it: it was written at top speed, amid the rush and press of my medical practice, without regard to time or method.... The urgency that lay behind it became clear to me only later: it was the explosion of all those psychic contents which could find no room, no breathing-space, in the constricting atmosphere of Freudian psychology and its narrow outlook.[14]

After explaining that he doesn't wish to "denigrate Freud," and after pointing out some merits of Freud's work, he explains that what was problematic for him in Freud was the

> reductive causalism of his whole outlook, and the almost complete disregard of the teleological directedness which is so characteristic of everything psychic.... [Freud's views] move within the confines of outmoded rationalism and scientific materialism of the late nineteenth century.[15]

Of course, to Freud the causalism, rationalism, and materialism that Jung criticized were the badges of honor of what Freud considered scientific thinking. Teleology, or the finding of purposes in causal and temporal relations, is something that Freud rejected. Now we have Jung's reasons for writing the book the first time.

Why, then, did he revise the book? Because it is only after years of investigating "unconscious processes" that he could discover "bit by bit, the connecting links" that he needed to know in order to fill in the gaps of what he considered a fragmentary book.[16]

"Some Instances of Subconscious Creative Imagination" by Miss Frank Miller

The immediate impetus for Jung's investigation was the article the title of which heads this section. Jung became aware of this article through his friend Théodore Flournoy. Miss Frank Miller was the pseudonym of a young American journalist returning from a tour of Europe. The article was published in a French translation in a 1906 issue of *Archives de Psychologie* with an introduction by Flournoy. Jung did not know that the English original was published the following year in *The Journal of the American Society for Psychical Research*. The short article, reprinted in Jung's *Collected Works*, is only fifteen pages long. Jung's discussion, however, runs 444 pages! "Some Instances of Subconscious Creative Imagination" is a compendium of visions, dreams, and "channeling" experiences. Her reason for writing her observations, she says, is

> that they may help others to free their minds from things of the same kind that are worrying them and do something to clear up the more complex phenomena that are often presented by mediums.[17]

Unfortunately, from what Jung says in the 1924 "Foreword to the Second (German) Edition," the author had a "schizophrenic disturbance which had broken out after her sojourn in Europe." Jung found this out in 1918 from the American therapist who treated her. He also learned that her therapist said that "even personal acquaintance with the patient had not taught him 'one iota more' about her mentality" than Jung had discovered in his analysis without ever having seen her.[18] It is this new information that prompted the addition of the book's subtitle in the later edition. In the "Epilogue" of Part II, Jung thinks that his book shows us that it is in "no sense sufficient to try to [understand the products of the unconscious] with nothing but a personalistically oriented psychology." A further requirement is that the therapist must have "some knowledge of anatomy, physiology, embryology, and comparative evolution," as well as the "anatomy and evolutionary history of the mind he is setting out to cure.[19]

The Break with Freud

Jung opens Part I of *The Symbols of Transformation* with an "Introduction" in which he explains the value of Freud's using the insights of his practice to throw light on the Oedipus legend. He lists a number of works in the Freudian vein that have provided "a clue to historical problems through the application of insights derived from the activity of the unconscious psyche in modern man." This holds not just for "historical products" but extends "with particular force to the symbolism."[20] For Jung, this does not extend far enough:

> For just as psychological knowledge furthers our understanding of the historical material, so, conversely, the historical material can throw new light on individual psychological problems. These considerations have led me to direct my attention more to the historical side of the picture, in the hope of gaining fresh insights into the foundations of psychology.[21]

What Freud could not accept was that Jung was extending the causal base for the human psyche beyond the individual's experience. That is, Jung was claiming that aspects of myths from the Greeks, Romans, Babylonians, early Germans, Egyptians, Native Americans, early Christians, *etc.*, can affect the individual or explain the individual's dreams and visions, even if the person has never consciously come in contact with the material! Describing the importance of this change, Joseph Campbell says in his introduction to *The Portable Jung*:

> It was this radical shift of ground from a subjective and personalistic, essentially *biographical* approach to the reading of the symbolism of the psyche, to a larger, culture-historical, *mythological* orientation, that then became the characteristic of Jung's psychology.[22]

As Jung puts it in Chapter IV of Part II, "The Origin of the Hero":

> The psychotherapist cannot fail to be impressed when he realizes how uniform the unconscious images are despite their surface richness.... The reactions and products of the animal psyche have a uniformity and constancy of which we seem able to discover only sporadic traces in man. Man seems to us far more individual than the animals. This may perhaps be a delusion...[23]

The second point Freud would be offended by is first mentioned in Chapter II of Part I, "Two Kinds of Thinking." Here Jung suggests that Freud's concern with sexual interpretation "leads to a 'monotony' of interpretation, of which he said Freud was aware.[24] Two pages earlier, he says that

> Sex, as one of the most important instincts, is the prime cause of numerous affects that exert an abiding influence on our speech. But affects cannot be identified with sexuality inasmuch as they

may easily spring from conflict situations—for instance, many emotions spring from the instinct of self-preservation.[25]

Freud finds his "scientific" psychology rejected along with his notions that it is the individual's past experiences, particularly the individual's sexual development, that has shaped the person's psychological situation. Jung, from then on, uses the word "*libido*" as a synonym for general psychic energy, as opposed to the Freudian usage which is limited to the sexual aspect: "it is not the sexual instinct, but a kind of neutral energy, which is responsible for the formation of such symbols as light, fire, sun, and the like."[26]

Autonomy

As is noted above, in the introductory material for this book Jung criticizes Freud's rejection of teleology. This is related to Jung's view of the complexes discussed earlier in this chapter. In *Symbols of Transformation*, Jung continues the development of his idea that the different parts of the psyche are autonomous and develop for some purpose. Early in Part I of the book, Jung states a tenet that he would hold the rest of his career: "the law of psychic causality is never taken seriously enough: there are no accidents, no 'just as wells.' It *is* so, and there is a very good reason why it is so."[27] Freud, too, held a view like this. In fact, this is what Freud had in mind when discussing dreams, jokes, and *parapraxes* (i.e., "Freudian slips"). For Freud and Jung, whatever manifests itself psychologically must be taken seriously. Science is limited, Jung says to studying these subjective complexes, there can be no objective truth about the reference of these ideas (what he will later call "archetypes"):

> This complex, as experience has shown, possesses a certain functional autonomy and has proved itself to be a psychic existent. That is what psychological experience is primarily concerned with, and to that extent can be an object of science. Science can only establish the existence of psychic factors, and provided that we do not overstep these limits with professions of faith, in all so-called metaphysical problems we find ourselves confronted exclusively with psychic existents.[28]

Further, he claims in the chapter, "Symbols of the Mother and of Rebirth," from Part II, that the symbols and figures are

> personifications of the libido. Now it is a fact amply confirmed by psychiatric experience that all parts of the psyche, inasmuch as they possess a certain autonomy, exhibit a personal character, like the split-off products of hysteria and schizophrenia, mediumistic

17

"spirits," figures seen in dreams, etc. Every split-off portion of libido, every complex, has or is a (fragmentary) personality... they manifest themselves as... personal agencies. In this form they are felt as actual experiences and are not "figments of the imagination," as rationalism would have us believe.[29]

Part of his defense of this passage is problematic, however. Jung defends this explanation of autonomy with this sentence: "There are no conclusive arguments against the hypothesis that these archetypal figures are endowed personality at the outset and are not just secondary personalizations."[30] This is problematic because you cannot prove that something *is the case* by claiming that no one has proved that *it is not the case*. This is the called the fallacy of "argument from ignorance" by logicians. This, too, is something that Freud would reject.

In addition, we have to realize that the unconscious is not under our direct control: "*the unconscious is nature, which never deceives: only we deceive ourselves.*"[31] For Jung, the religious and/or mythological elements in our unconscious "transcend consciousness," and we must accept that these "contents are real, that they are agents which it is not only possible but absolutely necessary for us to come to terms."[32] The goal for Jung is not scientific verification, but rather *understanding*. For, it is only through understanding that therapists can help their patients. The important thing is not whether Miss E. (mentioned above) really saw dead people, but instead that these images and events have a psychological reality.

Jung's Defense of his Method

Symbols of Transformation is important more for Jung's change in methodological emphasis than for its actual analysis. Miss Miller's problems are more of a springboard for Jung's developing approach. The book contains hints of the ideas of archetypes and the collective unconscious. These ideas will be considered in the next chapter. Sprinkled throughout the book are defenses of this new methodology. Some explanations of his view of autonomy have already been discussed.

There are also defenses of his extensive use of material from various mythological, religious, and literary traditions, as well as the study of word-derivation, etymology. It is this aspect of his exposition that accounts for the length of the book when compared to Miss Miller's article. Some of the discussions are prompted by Miss Miller's recollections of myths, poems, etc. Many more are Jung's elaborations of similar themes. Jung's defenses occur late in the book. In a chapter from Part II, "The Dual Mother," he addresses what he thinks might be the skepticism of his audience:

> My reader must frequently have wondered at the number of times I adduce apparently very remote material for purposes of comparison and how I enlarge the basis upon which Miss Miller's creations rest. He must also have doubted whether it is justifiable, on the basis of such scanty suggestions, to enter into fundamental discussions concerning the mythological foundations of these fantasies. For, he will say, we are not likely to find anything of the sort behind the Miller fantasies.... The information we obtain from our patients is seldom complete.... But, although instances of cryptomnesia are not uncommon, it is highly probable that not all our ideas are individual acquisitions.... Because the basic structure of the psyche is everywhere more or less the same, it is possible to compare what look like individual dream-motifs with mythologems of whatever origin. So I have no hesitation in making comparisons between American Indian myth and the modern American psyche.[33]

By the time one has reached this point in Jung's text, particularly if unfamiliar with Jung's later texts, one *will* have wearied of the accumulation of examples. Of course, it is up to the reader to decide whether or not to accept Jung's defense of his method and its results.

Jung is also at pains to explain his stance on religious material. When he is discussing what he calls "the psychology of religious figures" and comparing them to myths, fantasies, and visions, he is not claiming that they are of the same status metaphysically (that they refer to the same kinds of being, or beings), but only that they have the same standing psychologically. He admits that "from another point of view," the religious view, they "can hardly be compared at all."[34]

The last defense we need to consider is his defense of his interpretive method. In Chapter VII of Part II, he ties this issue back to the other topic discussed in this section:

> The only certain and reliable thing is that the myth exists and shows unmistakable analogies with other myths. Myth-interpretation is a tricky business and there is some justification for looking at it askance. Hitherto the myth-interpreter has found himself in a somewhat unenviable position, because he had only had exceedingly doubtful points for orientation at his disposal, such as astronomical and meteorological data. Modern psychology has the distinct advantage of having opened up a field of psychic phenomena which are themselves the matrix of all mythology—I mean dreams, visions, fantasies, and delusional ideas.[35]

19

Of course, one will only accept this argument, if you have already accepted the conclusion. Jung answers the question "Why should we accept the psychological application of myth?" with the answer that "Psychic phenomena are the 'matrix of all mythology.'" If you are not already convinced of what he wants to prove, you are unlikely to be convinced by his reason which is just a restatement of what he is arguing for in the first place. This is a variation of the logical fallacy known as "begging the question." As with his other defenses, it is up to the reader to decide which of his arguments and explanations to accept and which need to be rejected.

Notes

[1] "The Psychology of Dementia Praecox," in *CW*, vol. 3, pp. 1-151.

[2] "On the Psychology and Pathology of So-Called Occult Phenomena," in *CW*, vol. 1, pp. 3-88. *Symbols of Transformation* is *CW*, vol. 5.

[3] For more on these relationships, see Peter Gay's book (bibliography).

[4] "On the Psychology and Pathology of So-Called Occult Phenomena," in *CW*, vol. 1, p. 64.

[5] *Ibid.*, pp. 69-70.

[6] "On Hysterical Misreading," in *CW*, vol. 1, pp. 89-92.

[7] *Op. Cit.*, pp. 17-18.

[8] *Ibid.*, pp. 5-17.

[9] The papers on the association tests are in *CW*, vol. 2, pp. 3-491.

[10] For more on this, see Storr, *C.G. Jung*, pp. 21-23.

[11] "The Tavistock Lectures," in *CW*, vol. 18, p. 73.

[12] "Schizophrenia," in *CW*, vol. 3, pp. 256-272.

[13] Peter Homans makes a similar point in his *Jung in Context*, p. 27.

[14] *Op. Cit.*, p. xxiii.

[15] *Ibid.*

[16] *Ibid.*, pp. xxv.

[17] *Ibid.*, p. 462.

[18] *Ibid.*, pp. xxviii-xxix.

[19] *Ibid.*, pp. 442-443.

[20] *Ibid.*, p. 5.

[21] *Ibid.*, pp. 5-6.

[22] Campbell, "Editor's Introduction," in *The Portable Jung*, p. xxi. Campbell's emphasis.

[23] *Op. Cit.*, p. 176.

[24] *Ibid.*, p. 10.

[25] *Ibid.*, p. 8.

[26] *Ibid.*, p. 139.

[27] *Ibid.*, p. 146. Jung's emphasis.

[28] *Ibid.*, pp. 61-62.

[29] *Ibid.*, p. 255.

[30] *Ibid.*

[31] *Ibid.*, p. 62. Jung's emphasis

[32] *Ibid.*, pp. 77-78.

[33] *Ibid.*, pp. 312-313.

[34] *Ibid.*, pp. 367-368.

[35] *Ibid.*, p. 390.

3

The Development of Analytic Psychology

Introduction

Our discussion in this chapter moves to the views on human nature that Jung published upon emerging from his more or less silent, self-reflective period. This work was primarily concerned with the types of personalities, the components of the individual psyche and its relation to what he called the collective unconscious.

Psychological Types

In developing his delineation of personality types, Jung provided two levels of analysis. The first level is concerned with the individual's social attitude. Jung's basic division here is between the extravert and the introvert. The other division Jung made is at the level of what he called functions. This has to do with the dominance of differing aspects of mental activity. These four were thinking, feeling, sensation, and intuition. Any of these could be dominant within either the introvert or the extravert. Jung's division, then, provided eight basic psychological types. These distinctions, Jung tells us, derive from his experiences with patients and other people, and are therefore empirically grounded. He did not claim, however, that this list is exhaustive.

The Attitude Types: Extraversion and Introversion

In his book *Psychological Types*, Jung claims of this distinction that "it is not easy to characterize this contrasting relationship to the object in a way that is lucent and intelligible."[1] We shall keep Jung's warning in mind while attempting this difficult task. The introvert's orientation to the world always "sets the self and the subjective psychological process above the object and the objective process." The extravert, on the other hand, "sets the subject below the object, whereby the object receives the predominant value." He does not think, though, that anyone is ever completely extraverted or introverted. In fact, he thought that the individual might swing back and forth between these attitudes depending on life events. To Jung, they constitute "adaptation processes."

The Function Types: Thinking, Feeling, Sensation, and Intuition

Before seeing how these four functions affect the personality, it is important to lay out how Jung uses these terms as they do not exactly correspond to ordinary usage. For one thing, we must understand that Jung considers thinking and feeling to be rational functions, while sensation and intuition are irrational functions that do not require reason. All of the following can be found in the list of definitions at the end of *Psychological Types*.[2] Using Jung's exact words also provide you with a taste of his writing style. Also note that each of the full definitions I am excerpting from runs about two pages.

1. "Thinking is that psychological function which, in accordance with its own laws, brings given presentations into conceptual connection.... The term 'thinking' should, in my view, be confined to the linking up of representations by means of a concept, where, in other words, an act of judgment prevails, whether such an object be the product of one's intention or not."

2. "Feeling is primarily a process that takes place between the ego and a given content, a process, moreover, that imparts to the content a definite *value* in the sense of acceptance or rejection ('like' or 'dislike'); but it can also appear, as it were, isolated in the form of 'mood,' quite apart from the momentary contents of consciousness or momentary sensations.... Feeling, therefore, is an entirely *subjective* process, which may be in every respect independent of external stimuli."

3. "Sensation, or sensing, is that psychological function which transmits a physical stimulus to perception. It is, therefore identical with perception.... Sensation is related not only to the outer stimuli, but also to the inner, i.e., to changes in the internal

organs."

4. "[Intuition] is that psychological function which transmits perceptions *in an unconscious way*. Everything, whether outer or inner objects or their associations, can be the object of this perception. Intuition has this peculiar quality: it is neither sensation, nor feeling, nor intellectual conclusion, although it may appear in any of these forms. Through intuition any one content is presented as a complete whole, without our being able to explain or discover in what way this content has been arrived at. Intuition is a kind of instinctive apprehension, irrespective of the nature of its contents."

Each of these function types can only be fully understood when paired up with either the introverted or extraverted attitude type. First come the four extraverted types. The four introverted types will follow them.[3]

The *extraverted thinking* type is driven by the quest for objective knowledge. The scientist is often given as the example here. Thinking is usually stressed over feeling. The healthy extraverted thinker might be Einstein or Darwin. The pathological extraverted thinker represses feeling too much and might be represented by Dr. Jekyll or Victor Frankenstein.

The *extraverted feeling* type, Jung thinks, is most frequently found in women. People of this type are driven by their emotions and moods, which change as rapidly as do the situations they are in. The pathological type, in which thinking is repressed too much, has trouble developing intellectually.

The *extraverted sensation* type mostly occurs in men, according to Jung. This type likes to accumulate facts about the world or catalogues of sensations. They are practical and hardheaded, but particularly unconcerned with what things *mean*. Sensations, pleasures, and thrills are often eagerly sought to add to the catalogue of the world. Pathology here leads to addictions of various kinds. This type calls to mind the description Danish philosopher Søren Kierkegaard (1813-1855) gave of the aesthete who lives life moment-to-moment searching for the next exciting sensation.[4]

The *extraverted intuitive* type, which Jung thinks is primarily found in women, is "flighty" and unstable. Since thinking is de-emphasized, people of this type move from goal to goal without being able to achieve their aims. In other words, they are very good at getting excited by new projects but lack the "follow-through."

The *introverted thinking* type is equated by Jung with the philosopher and psychologist. This person likes to be alone and quietly

The Development of Analytic Psychology

thinking. The more that feeling is repressed here, the more irritable, unapproachable, and quixotic the person is liable to become. Jung thinks that schizophrenia might occur in the pathological case, as one totally withdraws from the external world.

The *introverted feeling* type, like its extraverted counterpart, is also found more commonly in women, in Jung's view. Their emotional patterns are more internalized than in the extraverts. Because of this they often appear mysterious. Since the feelings are not commonly expressed, the person of this type is prone to unexpected and stormy outbursts.

The *introverted sensation* type is found in people unconcerned with the world of external objects. That is, people who are likely to find internal sensations more appealing than the world. They are uncommunicative and often are failed artists and poets because of the extent to which thought and feeling (characteristics of great artists) are deficient.

The *introverted intuitive* type, on the other hand, includes successful artists, but also "dreamers, prophets, visionaries, and cranks."[5] The internal images (see the next section on archetypes) which are focused on are not well understood or communicated because of deficiencies in thinking. Often others will be able to bring their intuitions to fruition.

The Myers-Briggs Type Indicator

These insights have had much practical use in recent years. The very famous Myers-Briggs Type Indicator test makes use of Jung's types in trying to assess people's traits and abilities to work with each other. It was originally developed by Kathryn Briggs and her daughter Isabel Briggs-Myers. Through a series of questions it determines whether you are generally extraverted or introverted and which two of the four function types you are most likely to rely upon. Thus, in this test there are sixteen basic types. [6]

Archetypes

Although the word archetype is not the term first used by Jung to designate the concept we are about to consider, it is the one that is most well known. Perhaps it is the aspect of Jung's psychology that has most become part of the contemporary arsenal of concepts. It is not an easy term to explain, either. In his paper, "Archetypes of the Collective Unconscious," Jung describes the archetype as "an unconscious content that is altered by becoming conscious and by being perceived, and it takes its color from the individual consciousness in which it happens to appear."[7]   However, he immediately says that "if we try to establish what an archetype is psychologically, the matter becomes more complicated."   It is helpful to begin with the first phrase he used to describe this concept, "primordial image."   Initially Jung used this term to refer to the basic, primitive ideas that persist in the unconsciousness of individuals, but do not originate in their individual experiences.   In some sense, awareness of these primordial images is only activated when particular experiences reinscribe primitive experiences.   These archetypes he thought were universal and exist because of the formation of the human brain and human consciousness over time. There are many archetypes that Jung discusses in many works.   These are discovered by studying dreams in analysis and by studying the form and content of mythology.   The most important of these archetypes are described in what comes next.

The Self

The self is the organizing principle of the individual person.   Jung did not think we sprang from the womb as fully formed selves.   We develop over time, and through a process he calls individuation, we become who we are.   In *Psychological Types*, he describes the self as the empirical concept of the "unity of the personality of the whole."[8]   It can only be partly conscious because it contains what we are to become as well as what we have already experienced.   It most frequently appears in "dreams, myths, and fairy tales" as "a king, hero, prophet, savior, etc."[9]

This process of individuation can never be complete, though.   In order for it to be completed we would have to achieve a complete, perfect wholeness.   This can be seen by examining Jung's favorite example of the archetype.   The example Jung gives in his late work, *Aion*,[10] for the archetype of the self is Christ: "Christ exemplifies the archetype of the self.   He represents a totality of a divine or heavenly kind, a glorified man, a son of God..., unspotted by sin."[11]   During the process of individuation the unconscious produces images of totality. Jung considers these to be "spontaneous symbols of the self, or of wholeness."[12]   At the end of the chapter, Jung summarizes this way:

> The Christ-image fully corresponds to this situation: Christ is the perfect man who is crucified.   One could hardly think of a truer picture of the goal of ethical endeavour.   At any rate the transcendental idea of the self that serves psychology... can never match that image because, although it is a symbol, it lacks that character of a revelatory historical event....   the idea of the self is at least in part a product of cognition, grounded neither on faith

26

nor on metaphysical speculation but on the experience that under certain conditions the unconscious spontaneously brings forth an archetypal symbol of wholeness. From this we must conclude that some such archetype occurs universally...[13]

Since we cannot become Christ, the process cannot be completed.

Anima and Animus

The *anima* and the *animus* are the feminine and masculine aspects that reside in the unconscious of men and women, respectively. Both of these terms are derived from the Latin word for soul. A clear view of how Jung uses these terms can be seen from his summary discussion in, *Aion*. In *Aion*, he describes the anima as the maternal Eros (passion or love) in the male and the animus is the paternal Logos (reason or logic) in the female. For Jung, in the usual state of affairs

> woman's consciousness is characterized more by the connective quality of Eros than by the discrimination and cognition associated with Logos. In men, Eros, the function of relationship, is usually less developed than the Logos. In women, on the other hand, Eros is an expression of their true nature, while their Logos is often only a regrettable accident.[14]

This view, once made clear, explains Jung's views about women and psychological types earlier in this chapter. This passage also seems to imply that rational women are "a regrettable accident," which violates "their true nature." Many of Jung's discussions of women have similar themes. He does, however, say that this is "often" an accident, and he does not say it always is. From what he says in the immediately following sentence, the reason that Logos in women is regrettable is because women lack conceptual rigor, and so the Logos is employed in opinion, and not reflection. This has particularly bad consequences, Jung thinks, when men and women argue. I will quote extensively from *Aion* here, as Jung's own description most clearly makes manifest his attitudes toward the psychology of men and women.

> As the animus is partial to argument, he can best be seen at work in disputes where both parties know they are right. Men can argue in a very womanish way, too, when they are anima-possessed and have thus been transformed into the animus of their own anima. With them the question becomes one of personal vanity and touchiness (as if they were females); with women it is a question of *power*, whether of truth or justice or some other "ism"—for the dressmaker and hairdresser have already taken

care of their vanity. The "Father" (i.e., the sum of conventional opinions) always plays a great role in female argumentation. No matter how friendly and obliging a woman's Eros may be, no logic on earth can shake her if she is ridden by the animus. Often the man has the feeling—and he is not mistaken—that only seduction or a beating or rape would have the necessary power of persuasion.... [Further] no man can converse with an animus for five minutes without becoming the victim of his own anima.... [Anyone listening] would be staggered by the vast number of commonplaces, misapplied truisms, clichés from newspapers and novels, shop-soiled platitudes of every description interspersed with vulgar abuse and brain-splitting lack of logic. It is a dialogue which... is repeated millions and millions of times in all the languages of the world and always remains essentially the same.[15]

Jung seems to be assuming that there are unchanging essences for what it is to be a man or a woman, and that men and women just play out their given roles. There seems to be no hope for change. But, as Jung tries to explain why this happens, he seems to think that things perhaps aren't that bad after all:

when animus and anima meet, the animus draws his sword of power and the anima ejects her poison of illusion and seduction. The outcome need not always be negative, since the two are equally likely to fall in love (a special instance of love at first sight). The language of love is of astonishing uniformity, using the well-worn formulas with the utmost devotion and fidelity, so that once again the two partners find themselves in a banal collective situation.[16]

One might wonder if this falling in love occurs before or after the seduction, beating, or rape mentioned above!

The Shadow

Like the self, the shadow can be partially located in the personal rather than the collective unconscious. Jung calls the shadow "a moral problem that challenges the whole ego-personality."[17] The shadow usually appears as the same sex as the person, but in some sense "darker." To become aware of it we have to address and/or confront "the dark aspects of the personality as present and real." When trying to integrate the shadow into the personality, we have to accept that we, just as everyone else does, have such a dark side. This integration is difficult and will often produce resistance. This is particularly true if we associate our own shadow with the collective, rather than personal archetype. Then, as Jung says, "it is quite within the bounds of possibility for a man to recognize the relative evil of his nature, but it is a rare and shattering experience for him to gaze into the face of absolute evil."[18] Failing to integrate can lead to maladjustments such as obsessional or compulsional neurosis, as we become fixated on the shadow.

To return to the example of Christ as symbol of self discussed above, Jung considers the antichrist as an example of shadow. In a later chapter of *Aion*, he says that

> the Antichrist would correspond to the shadow of the self, namely the dark half of the human totality, which ought not to be judged too optimistically.... The psychological concept of the self... cannot omit the shadow... for without it this figure lacks body and humanity. In the empirical self, light and shadow form a paradoxical unity. In the Christian concept, on the other hand, the archetype is hopelessly split into two irreconcilable halves... [19]

Too much differentiation in one's consciousness can lead to a symbolic "crucifixion of the ego." For Jung, this further emphasizes the importance of coming to terms with the shadow through the individuation process.

The Wise Old Man and the Chthonic Mother

The meaning of the phrase wise old man is common enough. The word "chthonic" is not really in common usage any longer, but it refers to the underworld of the Greek gods. These are examples of motherly and fatherly archetypes.

It is not entirely clear in Jung to what extent the wise old man is derived from the personal or the collective unconscious and whether it is a general father figure or perhaps a god figure. Early in his life, Jung came to understand that there was an older authority figure or voice of experience embedded in his own personality. He called it his "No. 2" personality. During the self-reflective period discussed in Chapter 1 above, Jung started to call this wise old man Philemon (after a Gnostic thinker of the Hellenistic period).[20] The wise old man helps the personality deal with difficult mathematical problems or moral issues, for example, if you are patient and "sleep on it."

The chthonic mother, or as he sometimes called this archetype, the earth mother or the great mother is not as easy to deal with as the wise old man. Jung himself is not particularly clear. Those who would like to learn more about what Jung has to say about mother archetypes should look at the essay, "Psychological Aspects of the Mother Archetype."[21]

The Persona

The word "persona" is a Latin term that originated with the theater. It refers to the mask worn by performers. For Jung, the persona archetype, is a kind of mask we wear. Often, we try to identify ourselves with a role or profession, conform to societal expectations, or we can hide behind the mask, or put up a *façade* (false face). In short, the persona is "a functional complex that comes into existence for reasons of adaptation or personal convenience."[22] In a brief passage from *Archetypes of the Collective Unconscious*, Jung makes his most famous pronouncement on the persona:

> True, whoever looks into the mirror of the water will see first of all his own face. Whoever goes to himself risks a confrontation with himself. The mirror does not flatter, it faithfully shows whatever looks into it; namely, the face we never show the world because we cover it with the *persona*, the mask of the actor. But the mirror lies behind the mask and shows the true face.[23]

There are occasions when we rely too heavily on the persona. In these cases, which Jung calls inflation, our identification with the persona may make it more difficult to admit and address the issues connected with the shadow or lead to a feeling of inferiority about the self. In other cases, the attitude of the persona is "diametrically opposed" to the inner personality.[24] In *The Relations between the Ego and the Unconscious*, Jung says that the persona, as mask, merely

> *feigns individuality*, making others and oneself believe that one is individual, whereas one is simply acting a role through which the collective psyche speaks.... Fundamentally the persona is nothing real: it is a compromise between the individual and society as to what a man should appear to be.... The persona is a semblance, a two-dimensional reality, to give it a nickname.[25]

Examples of both useful and dangerous manifestations of the persona are easy to picture. People who struggle to fit in at the workplace may find that the only way to successfully display the proper professional attitude at work is to not let their own personality traits show. In order to do this, they may regulate themselves so much that they are no longer themselves at home. At this point the persona has taken over and is no longer a compromise or adaptation. This is frequently a problem that can be a result of the phenomenon of taking your work home with you.

An example of a somewhat more successful compromise can be seen in the life of Franz Kafka (1883-1924).[26] Kafka's short life is not usually offered up as an example of psychological well being, but he

managed to keep his workday persona separate from the creative writer
he was at home. At work, Kafka diligently performed his clerking job
at an insurance office in an orderly manner. No one would have
suspected that he was the author of the dream-like (or nightmare-like)
and disordered fiction that was published during his lifetime. The
characters in his stories, on the other hand, are not always as successful.
One way of reading Kafka's famous story, "The Metamorphosis," is as
the story of a man, Gregor Samsa, who has no life outside of work. As
the story begins, we find that

> One morning, upon awakening from agitated dreams, Gregor
> Samsa found himself, in his bed, transformed into a monstrous
> vermin. He lay on his hard, armorlike back, and when lifting his
> head slightly, he could view his brown, vaulted belly partitioned
> by arching ridges, while on top of it, the blanket, about to slide off
> altogether, could barely hold. His many legs, wretchedly thin
> compared with his overall girth, danced helplessly before his
> eyes.[27]

Gregor's first concern upon realizing he is a bug is to determine how he
is going to get to work as he is already late. Gregor's identification
with his persona predated his turning into a giant insect.

Existential philosophy and psychology also warns of the dangers
of the persona. In the phrase of the French philosopher Jean-Paul
Sartre (1905-1980), identification with the persona is "bad faith." That
is, when you act in bad faith you are treating yourself as a thing (a role,
a mask, an image) rather than as a person.[28] For Sartre, acting in bad
faith can be defined as "hiding a displeasing truth or presenting as truth
a pleasing untruth.... Only what changes everything is the fact that in
bad faith it is from myself that I am hiding the truth."[29] Sartre offers
two very vivid examples of bad faith in Being and Nothingness: a
woman on a date trying to decide whether or not to accept the advances
of her companion and a waiter trying to live up to his rôle.[30] The
waiter example is similar to the other examples discussed above. In a
café we find a waiter who is trying too hard: too polite, too stiff, and
walks too quickly. "We need not watch long," Sartre says, "before we
can explain it: he is playing at *being* a waiter."[31] This is true, though,
for all jobs. There is a public demand that the people playing these
rôles never show their humanity:

> A grocer who dreams is offensive to the buyer, because such a
> grocer is not wholly a grocer. Society demands that he limit
> himself to his function as a grocer just as the soldier at attention
> makes himself into a soldier-thing with a direct regard which does
> not see at all.... [But] the waiter in the café can not be

immediately a café waiter in the sense that this inkwell *is* an inkwell or the glass is a glass.[32]

This, then, is what constitutes bad faith: trying to become a thing, when you are not a thing. Bad faith is when I attempt to "constitute myself as being what I am not."[33] Sartre's notion of untruth here is parallel to the mirror example mentioned at the beginning of this section. Sartre, however, never accepted the Freudian notions of unconscious mental events and undoubtedly would have rejected Jung's discussion of archetypes. Yet, his discussion of the phenomenon of bad faith illustrates the same patterns of behavior.

The Collective Unconscious

In the last chapter we saw that Jung more or less accepted the Freudian analysis of the personal unconscious and that it was Jung's belief in the collective unconscious that in part precipitated the break with Freud. The personal unconscious, as you recall, contains events, memories, and wishes from the individual's existence. The collective unconscious, according to Jung, taps into the heritage of human experience. In what follows, we will consider what Jung means by this concept and what evidence he provides for its existence.

The Concept of the Collective Unconscious

The collective unconscious, Jung tells us, "as the ancestral heritage of possibilities of representation, is not individual but common to all men, and perhaps even to all animals." Although Jung's proof of this is delayed until the next section, there are some examples he uses to illustrate the concept. He mentions how the snake often functions in dreams in a mythological way that could not be derived from individual experience. That is, it comes from a "deeper level," a kind of "primitive mentality."[34] People can have snake-images appear in their dreams even if they have never seen a snake, a representation of a snake, or heard a description of a snake. He is aware that this concept is not going to be accepted by everyone so easily. When discussing the power of Christian symbolism he notes that

> The rationalist may laugh at this. But something deep in us is stirred, and not in us alone but in millions of Christian men and women, though we may call it only a feeling for beauty. What is stirred in us is that faraway background, those immemorial patterns of the human mind, which we have not acquired but have inherited from the dim ages of the past.[35]

It is right after this passage that Jung begins to provide the proof presented in the next section.

Evidence for the Existence of the Collective Unconscious

Although Jung rarely uses the language of proofs, in the case of the concept of the collective unconscious, he explicitly states in a number of places, that he has a proof for it. His proof is based on the experiences of an institutionalized paranoid schizophrenic, who frequently "believed himself to be the Savior." Jung came into contact with a man who told Jung that if you squinted when staring at the sun, you could see that the sun had a phallus, that the phallus was the origin of the wind, and if you moved your "head from side to side the sun phallus would move too." Jung describes this in his essay, "The Structure of the Psyche."[36] Jung tells us that the experience with the schizophrenic took place in 1906. In 1910, however, Jung becomes aware of a book by the classicist Dieterich that discussed a papyrus, which he took to contain rituals, visions, and liturgies of the ancient Persian Mithraic cults, which eventually made their way to Rome. Jung says of its contents

> One of these visions is described in the following words: "And likewise the so-called tube, the origin of the ministering wind. For you will see hanging down from the disc of the sun something that looks like a tube. And towards the regions westward it is as though there were an infinite east wind. But if the other wind should prevail towards the region of the east, you will in like manner see the vision veering in that direction."

Jung was quite taken aback by this. Even though Jung later became aware that Dieterich's book had been in a first edition in 1903, there was no way that his patient could have had access to this book. So, Jung rules out the possibility of cryptomnesia (buried memory). Is it possibly just a lucky coincidence between the patient and Mithraic cults? Not so, according to Jung because this wind-tube idea occurs in other mythology. For example, some medieval paintings depict a "hose-pipe reaching from heaven under the robe of Mary. In it the Holy Ghost flies down in the form of a dove to impregnate the virgin." Further the Holy Ghost is described in some texts as "a mighty rushing wind," and in one text it is said that "the spirit descends through the disc of the sun." From this Jung concludes that he

> cannot discover anything fortuitous in these visions, but simply the revival of possibilities that have always existed, that can be found again in the most diverse minds and in all epochs, and are therefore not to be mistaken for inherited ideas.

Jung does not discuss, however, whether there could have been cryptomnesia for the Christian version. This example is Jung's favorite proof, and he refers to it many places as the best proof of the existence of the collective unconscious.[37]

Notes

[1] *Psychological Types* comprises the entirety of *CW*, vol. 6. This quotation and the two that follow are from p. 5.

[2] *Ibid.*, pp. 408-466.

[3] The following examples are suggested by pp. 101-106 of Hall and Nordby, *A Primer of Jungian Psychology*.

[4] In particular, see his *Either/Or* and *Stages on Life's Way*.

[5] Hall and Nordby, p. 104.

[6] For a quick overview of how the Myers-Briggs test compares to Jung, see Platania, *Jung for Beginners*, pp. 56-57.

[7] "Archetypes of the Collective Unconscious," in *CW*, vol. 9. Part 1, p. 5, for this and the following quotation..

[8] "Psychological Types" in *CW*, vol. 6, p. 460.

[9] *Ibid.*

[10] Aion comprises the entirety of *CW*, vol. 9, part 2.

[11] *Ibid.*, p. 37.

[12] *Ibid.*, p. 40.

[13] *Ibid.*, p. 69.

[14] *Ibid.*, p. 14.

[15] *Ibid.*, p. 15.

[16] *Ibid.*, pp. 15-16.

[17] *Ibid.*, p. 8, for this and the following quotation.

[18] *Ibid.*, p. 10.

[19] *Ibid.*, p. 42.

[20] *Memories, Dreams, Reflections*, pp. 33-83, 170-199, 225.

[21] "Psychological Aspects of the Mother Archetype," in *CW*, vol. 9, part 1, pp. 75-110.

[22] "Psychological Types," in *CW*, vol. 6, p. 465.

[23] "Archetypes of the Collective Unconscious," in *CW*, vol. 9, part 1, p. 20.

[24] "Psychological Types," in *CW*, vol. 6, p. 467.

[25] "The Relations between the Ego and the Unconscious," in *CW*, vol. 7, pp. 157-158.

[26] This example is suggested by Hall and Nordby, pp. 44-45.

[27] Kafka, *The Metamorphosis and Other Stories*, p. 119.

[28] Sartre, *Being and Nothingness*, pp. 47-70, 557-585.

[29] *Ibid.*, p. 49.

[30] *Ibid.*, pp. 55-67.

[31] *Ibid.*, p. 59.

[32] *Ibid.*

[33] *Ibid.*, p. 67.

[34] "The Structure of the Psyche," in *CW*, vol. 8, pp. 147-148.

[35] *Ibid.*, pp. 149-150.

[36] *Ibid.*, pp. 150-151 for the preceding and succeeding passages of this section..

[37] Most notably, it also occurs in "The Concept of the Collective Unconscious," in *CW*, vol. 9, part 1, pp. 50-53.

4

Interlude: The Seminar on Nietzsche's *Thus Spake Zarathustra*

Introduction

At the request of his students at the Zürich Psychological Club, Jung began a seminar on Nietzsche's *Thus Spake Zarathustra* in May of 1934. The seminar continued until February 1939. Even then, after nearly five years, they did not make it all the way through Nietzsche's book! Of the 80 chapters in *Thus Spake Zarathustra*, the last chapter discussed in the seminar is Chapter 56, and Chapters 35-39, and Chapter 50 are skipped over. The *Zarathustra* seminar is the only time that Jung devoted his energies to what might be considered an explicitly philosophical text. The seminars met weekly on Wednesday mornings. There were eleven terms of seminars. Each term consisted of between seven to ten lectures, except the last term, which only contained five. There were 86 lectures in all.

Jung's Seminars

Jung's seminars for the Psychological Club, given in English, began at least as early as 1923. In 1925, the title was *Analytical Psychology*. From 1928-1930, they discussed *Dream Analysis*. In 1930 they began a long discussion of the *Interpretation of Visions*. In the middle of this discussion, in 1932, Jung conducted a seminar on *Kundalini Yoga*. The *Visions* seminar concluded in 1934. It was at this

The Seminar on Nietzsche's *Thus Spake Zarathustra*
point that the students requested a seminar on Nietzsche's *Zarathustra.*[1]
One feature of the seminars was that notes were copiously taken and
eventually the notes were distributed with the explicit warning that they
were only to be used for the education and edification of those
associated with Jung. In 1956, toward the end of his life, Jung granted
permission for the seminars to be published. In 1984, the *Dream
Analysis* volume was published. Volumes of the other seminars will be
forthcoming.

The full Nietzsche seminar (more than 1500 pages in two
volumes) was published in 1988, with an abridgement (376 pages in
one volume) following in 1998. It should be noted, though, that like
Symbols of Transformation (see Chapter 2), Jung's commentary is
much longer than the text he is considering. In the translation of
Zarathustra that Jung is using, the first 56 chapters amount to about
150 pages as compared to the 1500 of Jung's seminar!

Friedrich Nietzsche

Friedrich Wilhelm Nietzsche (1844-1900) was a Prussian
philosopher and philologist (expert in classical languages). Between
1869 and 1889 he published a number of books that were largely
reviled or ignored by his contemporaries. Many critics now consider
his works to prefigure important movements in Twentieth-century
thought. His views on self-realization and self-created values were
taken up by the existentialist movement, his views on the perspectival
nature of truth and the inescapable "prison-house" of language have
been extended by the Postmodernist movement. Nietzsche's writings
had an impact on a number of other thinkers as diverse as German
philosophers Karl Jaspers and Martin Heidegger, the historian Oswald
Spengler, creative writers Thomas Mann, Hermann Hesse, Rainer
Maria Rilke, George Bernard Shaw, and W. B. Yeats, the French
authors André Gide, Jean-Paul Sartre, and Albert Camus, and even the
theologians Nicholas Berdayev, Paul Tillich and Martin Buber.

What concerned Jung is that Nietzsche, like Arthur Schopenhauer
(1788-1860) before him, placed much of our mental functioning
beyond the reach of consciousness. The language that Nietzsche and
Schopenhauer used to describe the unconscious bears a resemblance to
language that would be used by Freud. Freud claimed in his
autobiography that he intentionally avoided the works of Nietzsche and
Schopenhauer so that he could independently arrive at scientific, or
empirical, results. This claim is difficult to take at face value as
Schopenhauer is mentioned frequently in Freud's writings.[2] Jung, on
the other hand, had read Schopenhauer and Nietzsche with much

interest. As was mentioned in Chapter 2, Jung made reference to Nietzsche's *Zarathustra* in his doctoral dissertation, even though Nietzsche is not given an extended treatment there.

Nietzsche's Thus Spake Zarathustra

Thus Spake Zarathustra was not published in its entirety, all at once. The four parts each came out separately. Parts I & II were published in 1883, Part III in 1884, and Part IV in 1885. Nietzsche's *Zarathustra* is a complicated work and is unlike anything else he published. Much of Nietzsche's other work is aphoristic in nature. That is, short gems of insight. *Zarathustra* is, on the other hand, a long sustained work. Also, it takes on the style of events in the life of religious leader. There was a real Zarathustra (the Greeks called him Zoroaster), but Nietzsche is not concerned with that.[3] The narrative reads much like works about Mahavira in Jain texts, Siddhartha Gautama in Buddhist texts, and the way Confucius is discussed in Confucian texts. Nietzsche's style in *Zarathustra* is much more poetic than his earlier or later texts, as well.

A helpful way of thinking about the book is to look at the different structural components to *Zarathustra*. First, Nietzsche is parodying the style of Scripture. Second, he is parodying the style of Plato. Finally, he is presenting Zarathustra as a tragic hero. The first two of these topics, which we can combine as the critique of the Christian/Platonic worldview, can be found in Nietzsche's other writings as well. In fact, Nietzsche often criticizes this worldview. He is particularly critical of Plato's dependence on reason and Christianity's denigration of the body.[4]

Zarathustra also contains development of two of Nietzsche's more famous doctrines: The Overman and The Doctrine of Eternal Recurrence. The Overman is Nietzsche's idea of a future humanity. The Overman would be the person who has moved beyond the man living in the Christian/Platonic worldview. The Doctrine of Eternal Recurrence is Nietzsche's reformulation of an idea that occurs in Ancient Greek philosophy. For Nietzsche it is a replacing of the linear view of time and history with a cyclical one. Although many disagree about how to interpret this view, one useful way of considering it is this: how would you act now if you thought that you would be repeating this exact event over and over again as life repeats itself? Underlying this would be the exhortation to affirm one's life in each of one's actions.

Another feature worth noting is that Zarathustra, like a tragic hero, always fails. On not even one occasion is Zarathustra successful in getting his idea across to the general public or his supposed followers. In fact, in a number of places, Zarathustra himself does not live up to his own doctrines. *Thus Spake Zarathustra* is not a simple work, and certainly the above-mentioned items are not the only aspects of *Zarathustra* that one could focus on, but this is a helpful way of addressing how the style and content of *Zarathustra* compare to his other writings.

The Seminar on Nietzsche's *Zarathustra*

Some authors, when writing books on Nietzsche, say more about their own thinking than they do about Nietzsche. This is true of the works on Nietzsche by Jaspers and Heidegger, and it is true of Jung's seminar as well.

Jung's treatment of *Thus Spake Zarathustra* is different than many other approaches. For one thing, Jung does not differentiate clearly between Nietzsche the author and *Zarathustra* the work. Jung reads the book as way of reading its author. For another, he does not treat the character Zarathustra as a character or tool for Nietzsche, but rather as a part of Nietzsche's psychology. In a number of places throughout the seminar, Jung explains and defends this attitude. In Lecture I from the Spring 1934 term, Jung says that much of *Zarathustra* reads like the visions on which they had just concluded a seminar. So, he tells his listeners that they will use the same techniques in studying Nietzsche that they used in analyzing the painted visions of Christina Morgan in the seminar that concluded two months earlier. During his discussion of the beginning of Nietzsche's book, Jung informs his group that

> The man who speaks or writes is Nietzsche; it is as if he were the historian of Zarathustra, describing what he had been doing. Zarathustra is obviously objectified here, the writer does not seem to be identical with him.[5]

However, Jung reminds us repeatedly that that in one of his poems, "Sils Maria," Nietzsche said of himself that he was sitting by the lake when "suddenly, friend, one became two—/And Zarathustra passed by me."[6] Jung takes this to mean that for Nietzsche, "Zarathustra then became manifest as a second personality in himself." In several places, Jung reads portions of Zarathustra as "prophecy, the unmistakable anticipation of the final catastrophe, his madness."[7] Here, Jung is referring to the fact that in 1889, only four years after completing *Zarathustra*, Nietzsche succumbed to a madness that kept him from normal functioning until his death in 1900. Jung justifies his attitude in Lecture III from the Spring Term of 1938:

Many a writer thinks his book is not himself, that it is objective, as if he were a god dismissing a world from his bosom...[8]

This is problematic for Nietzsche, Jung says, because it blinds Nietzsche to what he needs to do to solve his own problems. Instead, Nietzsche is unable to be honest with himself. Further, in Lecture I from Winter Term 1939, Jung says of reading philosophy that

> in reading a philosophy, it is not only the thought itself but the man that produced the thought that counts. Ask what it meant to him, for in reading those words you cannot help comparing them to what he himself was.... You see, from the context you could conclude here that a *condottiere* from the Renaissance, a hell of a fellow, was speaking. While in reality you find a kindly, very nervous, half-blind man who suffers from headaches and doesn't touch the world anywhere; he is up in a corner of a little house in the Engadine and disturbs not a fly.[9]

It is this attitude of Jung's that we must keep in mind when considering the Nietzsche seminar.

Much of the content of Jung's *Zarathustra* seminar is concerned with archetypes and individuation and with topics in religion. These two areas will be developed below first. After that, discussions of morality and politics follow. Given that the seminar is only recently published and not yet widely read, I will let Jung's lecture style speak for itself in much of what follows.

The Archetype of the Wise Old Man

It is clear from the beginning of the seminar that Jung thinks of Zarathustra as an instantiation of the archetype of the wise old man. In the first two lectures of the seminar he introduces this interpretation. In Lecture I, he just states this connection.[10] In Lecture II, he gives other examples of the wise old man ranging from the shaman or medicine man to the Catholic Pope. Jung discusses one of Nietzsche's letters to his sister, a letter describing the writing of *Zarathustra*, as proof of Zarathustra's being an example of the wise old man. He first discusses the archetype and only reads from the letter when prompted by his students. What Jung says is this:

> when God dies, man needs a new orientation. In that moment the father of all prophets, the wise old man, ought to appear to give a new revelation, to give birth to a new truth. That is what Nietzsche meant Zarathustra to be. The whole book is an extraordinary experience of that phenomenon, a sort of enthusiastic experience surrounded by all the paraphernalia, one

could say, of true revelation.[11]

This view is based on Nietzsche's claims in his letter that the composition of the book was "vehement," it happened "quite involuntarily," and that it had the character of revelation.[12]

The Archetypes of the Anima and Animus

The anima and animus archetypes are discussed throughout the seminar, as well. In Lecture II of Spring Term 1934, Jung says that one of the problems for Nietzsche is that his anima is not independent. The anima has to be involved, but

> the absence of the anima as an independent figure surely increases the weight of Zarathustra to a rather considerable degree. We have there a problem in itself, namely, the identity of Zarathustra with the anima, and most probably an identity of the author with the anima, so it is an extraordinary compound.[13]

Jung does not, however, further develop this line of thinking. He does in a later lecture from 1935 discuss the anima in a manner reminiscent of the way it was discussed last chapter. Again, it is worth quoting his words exactly here. Prompted by a discussion of mermaids and serpents he says:

> And that is the secret of the anima, human on one side and that most paradoxical and incomprehensible thing on the other. On the one side she is an inferior woman with all the bad qualities of a merely biological woman, an intriguing and plotting devil who always tries to entangle a man and make a perfect fool of him; yet she winds up with that snake's tail, with that peculiar insight and awareness. She... leads you into the understanding of the collective unconscious just by the way of the fool.[14]

When Jung says "an inferior woman" in this context, he means that for the male the anima is, or should be, the inferior figure. The rest, however, I think, must be taken at face value. There is no reference to Nietzsche in this passage.

The animus, as is usually the case with Jung, is not considered as much in the seminar as is the anima. Where the animus is discussed it is brought up in the context of a comment of Nietzsche's from Chapter 49 of *Zarathustra* where the masculinization of women is warned against. Jung's comment, similar to his description discussed in Chapter 3 above, is just a reminder that the animus is the masculine lurking in the unconscious of women. Jung also mentions the corresponding phenomenon, the feminization of men.[15]

The Archetype of the Shadow

Jung takes up the topic of the shadow archetype in Lecture VII from Spring Term 1934. Here his concern is with the concept of the Overman. The scene under discussion is "Zarathustra's Prologue." In it a rope-dancer is trying to walk across a tightrope while Zarathustra and a crowd are gathered beneath. Midway through his performance, a jester or buffoon jumps over the rope-dancer sending him to the ground below where he dies in Zarathustra's arms. In Jung's interpretation, the rope is the bridge to becoming the Overman, the rope-dancer is Nietzsche, and the buffoon is the shadow. In this case, the buffoon-shadow represents those people who prefer not to pass over the current human situation and fully flourish, and it is "a shadow whose power has been underrated."[16] Notice, again, that the discussion is more about Nietzsche than the text. In Lecture VII from Winter Term 1935, Jung reminds us that the shadow is the most difficult part of the personality to accept. This is because the shadow is

> the fact of one's own negation. For that other one in us is so utterly different from the conscious ego that one can say that it amounts to a negation of the ego, particularly when one is doubt which of the two ought to be; the shadow is so strong that you can honestly be in doubt as to what you really are.[17]

When you can assimilate the shadow, "you then appear to yourself not only subjective but as something objective as well."[18] There is, late in the seminar, another discussion of the shadow. In Lecture II of Autumn Term 1938, Jung talks about his preference for personifying the shadow. He says that it is only when the shadow is personified that the individual can succeed in "detaching the shadow."[19] You need to be able to do this so that you can distinguish yourself from the shadow. That is, you would no longer need to wonder if the shadow is the *real* you. This is not an easy task to accomplish. Nietzsche, according to Jung, to the extent that he is "identical with Zarathustra, he has the shadow problem."[20]

The Self and The Persona

Jung wants to explain his differences with Nietzsche regarding the self. For Jung, the self is a symbol. This is because it cannot be fully expressed. If it could be expressed, it would not be a symbol:

> It is a symbol, yet you can talk about it, you can explain it. But you can never explain what the self is, because the self in itself is unthinkable. Now that is not so here; to Nietzsche it is far more definite. He handles it as if it were explainable, and he identifies

it with the body...[21]

After this, Jung is questioned by his students at the beginning of the lecture. Talking scientifically about the self is difficult because it is a symbol. He tries to help them understand it with the help of an analogy:

> It is like trying to make a science of elephants, say. You can write a chapter in zoology about elephants, but to be actually under the feet of one is quite different. In the one case you are sitting in your study writing, and in the other you are in a damned unfortunate situation. That is so with the self. You talk about it in a perfectly friendly, scholarly way. Nobody is hurt. It is all nice and warm and afterwards you are going to eat your dinner. But if it should be an experience, well, you are just under the elephant.[22]

In addition to discussing the symbolic aspect of the self, he later considers the archaic elements of the self.

The self has both conscious elements (the ego) and unconscious elements. He says that the self

> consists, then, of the most recent acquisitions of the ego consciousness and on the other side, of the archaic material. The self is a fact of nature and always appears as such in immediate experiences, in dreams and visions, and so on... [it is] the great secret which has to be worked out.... It is also most dangerous... because it contains all the archetypes: one could say that an archetypal experience was the experience of the self.... The self makes terrible demands and can demand too much.[23]

Nietzsche's self is dealt with in Lecture I of Spring Term 1937. What Jung says here is very instructive as he ties the discussion of the self to the discussion of the other archetypes treated above. Of Nietzsche, he says

> it is perfectly clear that he is two, Nietzsche and Zarathustra. Nietzsche is "I," his ego, and the self is presumably Zarathustra.... Zarathustra, being the archetypal image of the wise old man naturally contains the self, as in all cases where that figure becomes a psychological experience.... So if you should say, "I am my Self," you would be neurotic, as Nietzsche was as a matter of fact, because he identified with Zarathustra. He would better say, "I am not the self, I am not Zarathustra."[24]

In the Winter Term of 1939, Jung discusses some relations between self and persona. In a way similar to the emphasis placed by Existentialists,[25] Jung states that we must accept that our fate is "in a way our choice all along." Since the world is as it is because of human psychology, "we can only conclude that whatever we meet with, inasmuch as it is man-made, is the thing we have chosen, the result of our particular psychology." It is difficult to bear this burden. The same thing goes for our persona as for the world around us. We can say that our persona was forced upon us, but it is really the case that you can only "blame yourself for taking on that persona, for allowing yourself to be poisoned by circumstances."[26]

Inflation and Individuation

Nietzsche became inflated. Jung's view of this is related to discussions of the relations between Nietzsche and Zarathustra discussed in preceding sections. Nietzsche, when writing the book

> was instantly filled with the inflation of Zarathustra: he became Zarathustra. Of course he knows all the time he is not Zarathustra—Zarathustra is a figure of speech.... If anybody asked him if he was Zarathustra he would probably have denied it. Nevertheless he handles Zarathustra—or Zarathustra handles him—as if they were one and the same.... So throughout the whole book we have had the greatest trouble on account of that constant intermingling with an archetypal figure. One is never sure whether Zarathustra is speaking, or Nietzsche—or is it his anima? This is not true, that is not true, and yet everything is true; Nietzsche is Zarathustra, he is the anima, he is the shadow, and so on.[27]

Nietzsche, though, did not have an analyst there to help him deal with his trouble. Nor does Jung think he would accept any treatment that was dependent on a view of the collective unconscious.[28]

In a number of the early parts of the seminar, Jung reads *Zarathustra* as Nietzsche's attempt to individuate, which is difficult to do if you are very different than your contemporaries. So, in Jung's view, the working out of all the archetypes discussed in preceding sections is Nietzsche suffering through the individuation process. That is why Zarathustra, the wise old man, is "so temperamental" and takes the form of a prophet. Nietzsche, according to Jung is "a mere instrument, a suffering body into which these powers are descended."[29] In *Zarathustra*, Nietzsche is trying to discover the meaning of individuation.[30]

Discussions of Religion

As Jung was increasingly concerned with the psychology of religion and religious symbols during the time the seminar was given, it is not surprising that there are a number of passages dealing with religious topics. Some of these issues, like his reading of the "Book of Job" and the two testaments as they appear in the Christian Bible, will be dealt with in the next chapter.

In two places in the Spring Term 1935 lectures, Jung says things about religious followers that aren't fully present in his other writings. In Lecture VII, he discusses Catholicism in the context of discussing large organizations. One comment that he makes is interesting. "The Catholics," he says, "surely fulfil an extraordinarily important task in that they keep so many of the unruly chaotic masses in check."[31] This is something Protestants can't do because of their lack of successful organization. Before this, in Lecture III, Jung discusses the neo-pagan Wotan movement that is associated with the political ideas of the Nazis. The word "Nazi" does not occur in the discussion, however. He is against the organizing of the neo-pagan movement into a formal structure. Individuals can have a "Wotan experience," as organization takes centuries of building; you cannot just create such an institution. In fact, for Jung,

> it would have been much better to leave the sheep to a well-organized church which is at least universal—that is the only redeeming factor in a church. But a national church, one that has a sort of pagan character, forebodes nothing good.[32]

This ties to his discussion of Catholicism in Lecture VII. Here, he explains that the usefulness of the organized church is that it can filter ideas to the masses, they can "paint things in becoming colors" which create "useful illusions" and thereby they can avoid many evils.[33] From these comments, it appears that Jung does not have much respect for the organizational aspects of religious traditions. This lack of respect, as we have seen, does not extend to the *ideas* in these traditions.

There are other short discussions that the reader can pursue. Lecture I of Winter Term 1936 contains a comparison of the attitudes of Christ and The Buddha regarding rejection of the world. There is a discussion of the scapegoat symbol in Lecture II of Spring Term 1936.

Discussions of Moral Psychology

Although there is no great detail in Jung's seminar, there are a few instances where Jung touches on issues of moral psychology. In Lecture II of Autumn Term 1935, Jung briefly provides his definition of free will: "You can only have free will—independent of environmental conditions of any kind—inasmuch as your consciousness is autonomous."[34] This is a more practical than

The Seminar on Nietzsche's *Thus Spake Zarathustra*
metaphysical definition. Jung considers free will to be a precondition for ethical behavior. That is, you need to be able to do otherwise. However, if your imagination outpaces your autonomy, you take on too much responsibility. Then you inflate like a balloon.[35] As Nietzsche rejects the notion of God as judge, Jung points out that the role of the judge must be taken into the self and the self is thus "in the same relation to the to us as the state is to the individual.... the whole is the judge."[36]

Jung discusses cruelty and power in two later lectures from 1936 and 1938. Of cruelty, Jung notes that it is something that gets passed down, or "inherited," in families. Part of the source of enjoying the torturing of others, he thinks, is the inability of people to enjoy themselves. People think that the only way to be moral is "to do something disagreeable to themselves" or "torture themselves."[37] Regarding power, Jung observes that those that strive for power are driven to "the power attitude" by their "feelings of inferiority."[38] This can create a vicious circle: the more one takes the power attitude, the more you feel inferior. This is the cause, for Jung, of Nietzsche's own preoccupation with the topic of power:

> He is blindfolded by his own complex, for he is the man who, on one side, has feelings of inferiority, and on the other, a tremendous power complex. What was the man Nietzsche in reality? A neurotic, a poor devil who suffered from migraine and a bad digestion.... Of course, all that contributed to the most beautiful inferiority complex you can imagine.[39]

Here again, Jung is concerned more with Nietzsche than his text.

The topic of virtue is discussed in Lecture I of Spring Term 1937. Jung observes that virtue is often "a cloak that covers up something else."[40] As with power, it is an attempt to mask one's own lack. Those who stress truth, honesty, or frankness are just those that have the urge to lie or conceal. In an interesting turn of phrase, Jung notes that when you are "digging up dirt you are quite close to the pig."[41] This implies that those that dig dirt get dirty themselves.

Nietzsche's concept of slave morality is briefly considered in Lecture VIII of Spring Term 1936. To Nietzsche, any time you define your values not by your own internal value system (master morality), but rather by some external source, whether it be religious or political, your will is enslaved (slave morality). Nietzsche considered Christianity to be a slave morality. Without mentioning the Nazis specifically (see below), Jung points out that the slave morality of Christianity can lead to the kind of "mob psychology" that is prevalent in the "complete destruction of political freedom in three countries

The Seminar on Nietzsche's *Thus Spake Zarathustra*
surrounding Switzerland."[42] Creating your own master morality has its
problems, too. In Lecture VI of Autumn Term 1938, Jung remarks that
the people wishing to have a master morality face two choices. On one
hand, they can follow their own path and risk being moral exiles, which
deprives them of the company of others. On the other hand, if they
give up their own judgment, then they become sheep. The sheep risks
becoming part of the mob mentioned above. This dilemma is
unavoidable. The only way to avoid neurosis is to view life as a
comedy, rather than as a tragedy. Unfortunately, according to Jung,
this understanding only comes in the second half of life.[43]

Discussions of Political Reality at the Time of the Seminar

Given that the seminar was meeting during the rise of Nazism,
one would expect that at some point there would be some discussion of
the political reality of Europe. There are very few references to the
political climate and no mention of Nazis by name. Even when asked
questions, Jung does not discuss the matter in any detail. Much of the
time the discussion is related back to the discussion of Wotan
mentioned above.

In Lecture III of Spring Term 1936, for example, Jung points out
the Wotan/pagan influence on explanations of German behavior in
World War I. When the Chancellor of Germany, Bethmann-Holweg,
was questioned regarding the invasion of Belgium, which broke a
treaty, his response included the explanation that "the Germans were
only pagans anyway."[44] From there he bemoans again the spread of
Wotan imagery.[45] In Lecture II of Spring Term 1936, Jung again
discusses the mob psychology aspects of German resurgence. In this
case he talks about the participation felt during ceremonies involving
shouting and brass bands that take on the appearance of a "primitive
collective religious phenomenon."[46] Right after he says this a member
of the seminar, a Mrs. Volkhardt, tells a story about how someone met
the Führer (Hitler), and found him "so very nice that she suddenly
fainted away."[47] Jung responds by changing the subject back to
Nietzsche without addressing her comment.[48] Another case of Jung
deflecting discussion occurs in Lecture V of Winter Term 1939. Jung
is discussing how the Germany of Nietzsche's time "suffered from the
weight of the past."[49] After Jung's statement, another member of the
seminar, Mrs. Flower, says that "this new analysis gives a frightful
picture of what is going on in Germany, in being only one-sided when
trying to get rid of the past."[50] Jung's response is to mention, instead,
that Russia is a better example. He then speaks about overthrowing
tradition in general, but does not address Mrs. Flower's comment.[51] As

48

The Seminar on Nietzsche's *Thus Spake Zarathustra* mentioned in Chapter 1, the reader will need to consult the biographies in the bibliography in order to reach any conclusions about Jung's attitudes on these matters.

Notes

[1] The seminar used the 1911 Thomas Common translation listed in the bibliography.

[2] Freud's comment is in Chapter V of his *An Autobiographical Study*, in vol. 20 of *The Standard Edition*. For more on this issue, see the Bilsker article listed in the bibliography and the references it contains.

[3] For more on the real Zarathustra and his doctrines, see Masani, *Zoroastrianism*. Jung addresses the issue of the real Zarathustra at the beginning of the seminar, *Jung's Seminar on Nietzsche's* Zarathustra, abridged edition, pp. 3-9.

[4] A similar line of thinking can be found in Kathleen Higgins' "Reading Zarathustra."

[5] *Op. Cit.*, p. 11.

[6] *Ibid.*, pp. 9-10, for this and the next quotation.

[7] *Ibid.*, p. 69.

[8] *Ibid.*, p. 316.

[9] *Ibid.*, p. 350. A "condottiere" is a leader of mercenary troops.

[10] The language Jung uses here is similar to language he will use when describing his own "wise old man" in his autobiography, *Memories, Dreams, Reflections*. Jung calls his wise old man his "No. 2" personality. See also Chapter 3 above.

[11] *Op. Cit.*, p. 24. The reference to God's death refers to one of Nietzsche's doctrines that is too involved to be discussed in this work.

[12] *Ibid.*, pp. 24-25. See also pp. 84-86, 215, 287.

[13] *Ibid.*, p. 30. See also pp. 267-268, 286-287.

[14] *Ibid.*, p. 175. See also pp. 322-324.

[15] *Ibid.*, p. 323.

[16] *Ibid.*, p. 61. See also pp. 165-168. It should also be noted that Jung uses "Superman," rather than "Overman." "Overman" is the more literal translation.

[17] *Ibid.*, p. 108.

[18] *Ibid.*, p, 109.

[19] *Ibid.*, pp. 333-334.

[20] *Ibid.*, pp. 334-335.

[21] *Ibid.*, p. 111. See also pp. 122-123.

[22] *Ibid.*, p. 132.

[23] *Ibid.*, pp. 240-241.

[24] *Ibid.*, p. 267.

[25] See the discussion of "bad faith" in Chapter 3 above.

[26] *Op. Cit.*, pp. 355-357, for this and the previous brief quotations.

[27] *Ibid.*, p. 331.

[28] For a fictionalized account of Nietzsche in therapy with Freud, see the novel, *When Nietzsche Wept*, by the psychologist Irwin Yalom.

[29] *Ibid.*, pp. 31-32.

[30] *Ibid.*, 52-53, 55.

[31] *Ibid.*, p. 145

[32] *Ibid.*, p. 142. See also pp. 237-238.

[33] *Ibid.*, p.145.

[34] *Ibid.*, p. 167.

[35] *Ibid.*

[36] *Ibid.*, p. 173. This is from Lecture VII of Autumn Term 1935. For more on the notion of internalizing the judge, see the Bilsker article listed in the bibliography.

[37] *Ibid.*, p. 235. This is from Lecture IV of Spring Term 1936.

[38] *Ibid.*, p. 307. This is from Lecture I of Spring Term 1938. See also pp. 337-338.

[39] *Ibid.*

[40] *Ibid.*, p. 262. See also pp. 329-330.

[41] *Ibid.*

[42] *Ibid.*, p. 252.

[43] *Ibid.*, pp. 338-341.

[44] *Ibid.*, p. 195. I am quoting Jung directly, who, in turn, is paraphrasing the Chancellor.

[45] *Ibid.*, p. 196. See also pp.237-238 for more on the resurgence of Wotan as an unconscious archetypal experience.

[46] *Ibid.*, pp. 225-226.

[47] *Ibid.*, p. 226.

[48] *Ibid.*, pp. 226-227.

[49] *Ibid.*, p. 373.

[50] *Ibid.*, p. 374.

[51] *Ibid.*, pp. 374-375.

5

Religion, Alchemy, and Mythology

Introduction

In his later years, Jung focused almost exclusively on the topics that comprise the title of this chapter. We have seen in earlier chapters that these themes have appeared in Jung's works throughout his career, beginning with his dissertation. Although it is generally the ideas of Chapter 3 that cemented Jung's importance for the history of psychology, it is the ideas of this chapter that have become increasingly popular in recent years as an influence on the "new age" and self-help movements.

Religion

As we have already seen, religious ideas play an important part in much of Jung's work. In this section, the focus is on two works. The first is the book *Psychology and Religion*. The contents of this book were originally given as the Terry Lectures at Yale University in 1937. In 1937, as was mentioned last chapter, Jung was in the middle of leading his five-year seminar on Nietzsche's *Zarathustra* to the Zürich Psychological Club.[1]

The second work to be discussed in this section is the book *Answer to Job*. *Answer to Job* was first published in 1952. It is an extended commentary on what Jung sees as the primary problems in interpreting *The Book of Job* from the Hebrew Testament.[2] In the course of the analysis, Jung considers elements of both testaments of the Christian Bible as well as the Pseudepigrapha[3] and Gnostic writings.

After discussing these two important texts, there will be a brief consideration of Jung's writings on Eastern religion. These short essays and forewords to other writers' books were published between 1936 and 1954. So, these are contained in the same time period as the other texts mentioned in this section and the rest of this chapter.

The Terry Lectures

Jung rarely provided digests of his work, preferring to let the works speak from themselves. The Terry lectures in their book form, *Psychology and Religion*, do serve as a general introduction to Jung's later views. This is primarily because Jung wanted his audience to have some context for his lectures.

At the beginning of his first lecture, "The Autonomy of the Unconscious Mind," Jung tells his audience (twice) that he is approaching the subject of religion as an empirical scientist, not as a philosopher. What he means by this is that he acknowledges religion as a psychological fact. It is a fact that people have their particular religious beliefs, visions, *etc*. This does not mean that he thinks that the *objects* of belief are factual. The subject matter of psychology is "ideas and other mental contents as zoology, for instance, deals with the different species of animals."[4] Jung uses the concept of the numinous to explain what he means by religion. This concept is due to the theologian Rudolf Otto. The numinous is that awesome mystery (*mysterium tremendum*) that compels belief. He contrasts this with a creed. A creed is a set of codified dogma, whereas religion concerns "the attitude peculiar to a consciousness which has been changed by experience of the *numinosum*."[5] As a psychologist, Jung is not concerned with "any creed, but the psychology of the *homo religiosus*,[6] the man who takes into account and carefully observes certain factors which influence him and his general condition."[7] After introducing his attitude toward religion, Jung moves on to the topic that makes up the title of the lecture. He summarizes his views of the autonomy of the complexes and the results of the association tests. From there, he is concerned to explain his approach to the collective unconscious. In a rather concise manner, Jung justifies this move as follows:

> It is, to my mind, a fatal mistake to consider the human psyche as a purely personal affair and to explain it exclusively from a personal point of view. Such a mode of explanation is only applicable to the individual in his ordinary everyday occupations and relationships. If, however, some slight trouble occurs,

perhaps in the form of an unforeseen and somewhat unusual event, instantly instinctual forces are called up, forces which appear to be wholly unexpected, new, and strange. They can no longer be explained in terms of personal motives, being comparable rather to certain primitive occurrences like panics at solar eclipses and the like.[8]

After this, Jung moves on to a discussion of the contents of dreams. He mentions that the study of dreams provides us with the same "conflicts and complexes" that we find verified by the association tests.[9] He also provides a quick explanation of how his approach to dream interpretation differs from Freud. Whereas Freud distinguishes between surface (manifest) meaning and deep (latent) meaning for dreams, Jung sees no reason to assume that the dream is devised to deceive us. He says he prefers to

> take the dream for what it is. The dream is such a difficult and intricate subject, that I do not dare to make any assumptions about its possible cunning. The dream is a natural occurrence and there is no earthly reason why we should assume that it is a crafty device to lead us astray.... It seems to be a natural product which is also found in people who are not neurotic.[10]

So, when a dream speaks of religion, he sees no reason not to take that seriously. Jung also reiterates the characteristics and importance of anima and animus figures in dreams and how they "personify the unconscious and give it its peculiarly disagreeable or irritating character."[11]

In the second lecture, "Dogma and Natural Symbols," Jung moves to connect the topics of the first lecture to his idea of archetypes more fully. In the course of this discussion, there are a few notable ideas. Returning to the idea of the autonomy of the unconscious, Jung says that "the unconscious is capable at times of manifesting an intelligence and purposiveness which are superior to the actual conscious insight."[12] This superiority is usually exhibited in dreams. Dreams, he adds, "are made of collective material to a very high degree."[13] The collective material is the instantiation of archetypes. Towards the end of the second lecture he addresses the existence of God. Recalling his attitude toward religion from the first lecture, Jung tells us that the occurrences of god-images in dreams do not signal a proof of God's existence. Rather, they

> prove only the existence of an archetypal God-image, which to my mind is the most we can assert about God psychologically. But as it is a very important and influential archetype, its

Religion, Alchemy, and Mythology

relatively frequent occurrence seems to be a noteworthy fact for any *theologia naturalis*.[14] And since experience of this archetype has the quality of numinosity, often in very high degree, it comes into the category of religious experiences.[15]

At the end of the lecture, Jung is comparing the symbols of trinity and quaternity as they occur in patients' dreams and visions and religious dogma. The third and final lecture, "The History and Psychology of a Natural Symbol," is concerned, in particular, with this quaternity symbol.

In this final lecture, Jung wants to show the collective nature of this symbol by connecting its occurrence in alchemy and Gnosticism with its occurrence in the dreams and visions of one of his patients. This method of discussion was previously mentioned in Chapter 3.

At the beginning of the lecture, Jung addresses what he considers might be a side effect of his analysis on his audience:

> While we are not concerned here with psychotherapy, but with the religious aspect of certain psychic phenomena, I have been forced through my studies in psychopathology to dig out these historical symbols and figures from the dust of their graves. When I was a young alienist[16] I should never have suspected myself of doing such a thing. I shall not mind, therefore, if this long discussion on the quaternity symbol... and the heretical attempts to improve on the dogma of the Trinity seem to be somewhat far-fetched and exaggerated.[17]

Later, he tells us that the discussions of alchemy (both medieval "Western" and Chinese) and gnosticism were important in order to put his "psychological observations into their historical setting," without which "they would remain suspended in mid air, a mere curiosity."[18] The technical discussion of the quaternity will be addressed in the next two sections of this chapter.

There are other important passages on religion in general that occur in this lecture. Religion, Jung says,

> is a relationship to the highest or most powerful value, be it positive or negative. The relationship is voluntary as well as involuntary, that is to say you can accept, consciously, the value by which you are possessed unconsciously. That psychological fact which wields the greatest power in your system functions as a god, since it is always the overwhelming psychic factor that is called "God." As soon as a god ceases to be an overwhelming factor , he dwindles to a mere name.[19]

This connects his definition of religion in terms of the numinous ("the overwhelming," in this case) to the issues of the coming-to-be and passing-away of religions.

He ends the lecture series by reminding us of our limitations:

> No one can know what the ultimate things are. We must therefore take them as we experience them. And if such experience helps to make your life healthier, more beautiful, more complete and more satisfactory to yourself and to those you love, you may safely say: "This was the grace of God."[20]

Ultimately, then, Jung stresses the therapeutic function of religion. In this way, Jung's Terry Lectures are similar to the views expressed by William James (1842-1910) in his "Gifford Lectures" at the University of Edinburgh.[21] James wished to explore the empirical, psychological effects religion had on people.

Answer to Job

Jung's *Answer to Job* is a fairly controversial book. One of the reasons for the controversy is that the book can be read as a psychological case study of the Judeo-Christian God. Job, a figure in the Hebrew Testament, was chosen as the subject of a bet between God and Satan.[22] The issue is whether God's faithful servant will remain faithful if catastrophe after catastrophe befalls him.[23] After Job passes his test, he is restored, by God, to his previous condition and then some. Before this though, he is given over to pain and disease, the death of his children, thefts and deaths of his cattle, and spurning by his wife, neighbors, friends, and family.

When a second edition in English of *Answer to Job* was published in 1956 for the Pastoral Psychology Book Club, Jung added a "Prefatory Note" to precede the preface ("Lectori Benevolo") that was already in place. In this note, Jung tells us what his aim was with the book. He is concerned with what has traditionally been called "the problem of evil." That is, the problem of reconciling the existence of God and the existence of evil. Jung puts it this way:

> If Christianity claims to be a monotheism, it becomes unavoidable to assume the opposites as being contained in God. But then we are confronted with a major religious problem: the problem of Job. It is the aim of my book to point out its historical evolution since the time of Job down through the centuries to the most recent symbolic phenomena, such as the *Assumptio Mariae*, etc. [24]

If God is one, then Satan is not equal in power to God, and the question of how evil originates still remains. Jung is troubled by the story of Job also because Job "expected help from God against God."[25] Job never gives up his faith in God and pleads for relief even when his friends assume that he must have done something to deserve his harsh and ever-worsening condition. Finally, at the end of the note, Jung informs us that with *Answer to Job* he

> wanted to avoid the impression... of announcing an "eternal truth." The book does not pretend to be anything but the voice or question of a single individual who hopes or expects to meet with thoughtfulness in the public.[26]

In addition to these comments, in the "Lectori Benevolo" he is aware of the controversy that his book his likely to engender. He reiterates his view of the psychological fact of religion discussed above in connection with *Psychology and Religion.* He says here that "religious statements... refer without exception to things that cannot be established as physical facts."[27] Even though they have this character, Jung does claim that there must *something* behind these ideas because they all can be reduced to a limited number of archetypal forms. Then he repeats what he said in *Psychology and Religion* about God-images.

The last prefatory comments he makes before he starts the twenty numbered sections of his analysis are concerned further with his goal for the book. He tells us that he is writing to understand what the Book of Job can mean to the contemporary Christian mind. He wants to learn "why and to what purpose Job was wounded, and what consequences have grown out of this for Yahweh as well as for man."[28] Note here that he talks about the consequences of the Job story *for* God. That is, that God is *changed* by the encounter with Job.

The twenty sections of *Answer to Job* move from the Book of Job which occurs toward the end of the Hebrew Testament through some of the rejected books of the Hebrew Testament (The Pseudepigrapha), and on through the Greek Testament up to Revelations. Jung wants to address a number of issues here. One is the question of why God needed to be incarnated as Jesus. Another is how the peaceful Jesus of the gospels can be reconciled with the fire-and-brimstone Jesus of Revelations. He is also, once again, interested in the quaternity. In this case, how the then new dogma of the Assumption of Mary can be interpreted as a change of the Trinity into a quaternity. Before he deals with these issues he has to deal with the concept of justice and what he calls the unconsciousness of Yahweh.

How can Job expect justice in his pleadings with God? Who could possibly be Job's advocate? Instead of allowing Job to plead his case at the end of the Book of Job, when he is speaking to him through a storm, God berates Job for wishing to question him. God basically says to Job, "How dare you!" As Jung states:

Yahweh does not think of bringing this mischief-making son [Satan] of his to account, nor does it ever occur to him to give Job at least the moral satisfaction of explaining his behaviour. Instead, he comes riding along on the tempest of his almightiness and thunders reproaches.[29]

This brings us, according to Jung, to the question of God's unconsciousness. Regarding the arrangement between God and Satan, how can God not know the result of such a test before it takes place? God's omniscience would seem to rule out any surprise. As God yells at Job for seventy-one verses (Job 38:1-40:2, 40:7-41:26), Jung is not sure what God is trying to accomplish. Job already accepts God's power. This is clear from Job's awareness of his situation. Job was only questioning why he was in his situation. To this God never responds. Given God's omniscience, he should have known this already, too. Jung reasons that God must have had another purpose for these verses:

> Job is no more than the outward occasion for an inward process of dialectic in God. His thunderings at Job so completely miss the point that one cannot help but see how much he is occupied with himself.... Yahweh must have seen that Job's loyalty was unshakable and that Satan had lost his bet.... Job has no alternative but formally to revoke his demand for justice.[30]

This is exactly what Job does as he covers his mouth and offers no response. Job's backing down had the effect of calming God down, according to Jung. For, after Job backs down God chastises the friends of Job who had abandoned him and gives Job new children and new herds of twice the size of the earlier ones. Job, as are all humans, is in "an impossible position," for Yahweh "on the one hand tramples on human life and happiness without regard, and on the other hand must have man for a partner."[31]

From here, Jung starts the process of moving from the story of Job to the incarnation of God as Jesus. For Jung, the "real reason for God's becoming man is to be sought in his encounter with Job."[32] First, Jung asks again about the need for the incarnation. If God is everywhere in creation, why incarnate? If Jesus were to redeem us from evil, wouldn't it be simpler for God to get rid of all evil by getting rid of Satan, or preventing him from doing evil? This, Jung claims, would seem to be much simpler than becoming human, having an immaculate conception and virgin birth, *etc.*[33]

God must incarnate because he has become conscious of Job's moral superiority: "Yahweh must become man precisely because he has done man a wrong."[34] This consciousness could only come because of

Satan's wager, says Jung. Jung states concisely the impetus for the incarnation.

> To sum up: the immediate cause of the incarnation lies in Job's elevation, and its purpose is the differentiation of Yahweh's consciousness. For this a situation of extreme gravity was needed,... without which no higher level of consciousness can be reached.[35]

After pointing out similarities between Christ and other examples of what he calls "the birth of a hero"[36] stories, Jung further explains the relationship between Job, Yahweh, and Christ. When Christ is on the cross, he finally understands what it means to suffer as Job suffered. This Jung calls "the answer to Job."[37] He relates this to archetypes by saying

> It is perfectly possible, psychologically, for the unconscious or an archetype to take complete possession of a man and to determine his fate down to the smallest detail.... My own conjecture is that Christ was such a personality. The life of Christ is just what it had to be if it is the life of a god and a man at the same time. It is a *symbolum*, a bringing together of heterogeneous natures, rather as if Job and Yahweh were combined in a single personality. Yahweh's intention to become man, which resulted from his collision with Job, is fulfilled in Christ's life and suffering.

It is important to remember Jung's prefatory warnings. He is not claiming to be a biblical scholar, he is merely trying to explain these stories psychologically based on his experiences of the relationships between individual and collective elements in the human psyche. You can see, however, why his comments and the way he states them would be considered controversial. This is especially true if his warnings were ignored and the book were read as providing anything other than a psychological reading. After two sections that deal, respectively, with the concepts of the Antichrist and the Holy Ghost, Jung moves on to the doctrine of salvation after the death of Christ.

As mentioned above, Jung is concerned to understand the idea of salvation through Christ in light of God's omniscience. Jung asks the questions in this way:

> What kind of father is it who would rather his son were slaughtered than forgive his ill-advised creatures who have been corrupted by his precious Satan? What is supposed to be demonstrated by this gruesome and archaic sacrifice of the son? God's love, perhaps? Or his implacability?[38]

Jung reminds us that sacrificing sons is a not an unknown theme

Religion, Alchemy, and Mythology
in the Hebrew Testament. In Genesis (22:1-19), Abraham is asked to sacrifice his son Isaac. In Exodus (22:29), in the rules listed after the Ten Commandments, God asks the Israelites for their first-born sons. In these places, too, God's omniscience should rule out the need for tests of faith. If Christ's sacrifice is to save humanity, the question, again, is "from what?" Jung says that what God does is "in the shape of his own son, to rescue mankind from himself."[39] Jung then considers how this differentiation in Yahweh's consciousness is prefigured in other biblical writings: Ezekiel and Daniel from the Hebrew Testament and Enoch[40] from the Pseudepigrapha. All these books contain prophecies and visions (including the quaternity), and therefore fit in with Jung's penchant for archetypal analysis. Ezekiel and Daniel are emphasized in Christianity because of their prophetic nature. Jung, however, spends more time on Enoch. At the end of the discussion, Jung uses the prefigurations as evidence that the way for Christianity had been paved by the existing historical structures. Jesus' actual teachings need to be addressed in Jung's analysis.

Christ's teachings about God as loving father, in particular, raise some of the same problems discussed above. Jung reminds us once again of the "insufferable incongruity" that

> this supremely good God only allows the purchase... of an act of grace through a human sacrifice, and what is worse, through the killing of his own son.... One should keep before one's eyes the strange fact that the God of goodness is so unforgiving that he can only be appeased by a human sacrifice![41]

But the sacrifice is not enough. God is still unconscious according to Jung. For Satan is still out there, he remains unpunished. Jung points out that

> In spite of all his misdeeds and in spite of God's work of redemption for mankind, the devil still maintains a position of considerable power and holds all sublunary creatures under his sway.... [this] does not correspond to what could reasonably have been expected from the "glad tidings." Evil is by no means fettered.... God still hesitates to use force against Satan. Presumably he still does not know how much his dark side favours the evil angel. Naturally this situation could not remain indefinitely hidden from the "spirit of truth" who has taken up his abode in man. He therefore created a disturbance in man's unconscious and produced... another great revelation.... This is the Revelation of St. John.[42]

This revelation, which Jung analyzes for most of the remainder of

Answer to Job, is the end of the Greek Testament that foretells the apocalyptic end of time. The revelation came to John in a vision: "the revelation of Jesus Christ... made known by sending his angel to his servant John."[43]

In the first part of his analysis, Jung is concerned with the relationship between the author of the revelation and its subject matter as well as the relationship between the Jesus that appears here and the Jesus that appears in the four gospels that open the Greek Testament. Jung singles out a number of the characteristics of Jesus in the Revelation that seem out of place. Jung points out that John describes Jesus as having a double-edge sword coming out of his mouth (1:16). Jung comments that this "would seem more suitable for fighting and the shedding of blood than for demonstrating brotherly love."[44] Right after this John describes Jesus' messages for the seven churches. Five of these messages are negative and contain warnings (2:1-3:22). The language of these messages is very violent. Christ warns and threatens these churches in a manner that Jung says is befitting "a bad-tempered, power-conscious 'boss' who very much resembles the 'shadow' of a love-preaching bishop."[45] Similarly, after discussing similarities between John's vision and images from Greek and Indian mythology, Jung returns to John's picture of Christ and its relation to John's psyche:

> His Christ-image, clouded by negative feeling, has turned into a savage avenger who no longer bears any real resemblance to a saviour. One is not at all sure whether this Christ-figure may not in the end have more of the human John in it, with his compensating shadow, than of the divine savior whom as the *lumen de lumine*, contains "no darkness".... We can turn it and twist it as we like, but, seen in the light of the gospel of love, the avenger and judge remains a most sinister figure.[46]

Jung explains John's situation of combining mythologies as caused by his visions having come from the collective unconscious. These visions can be described "too much in collective and archetypal forms for us to reduce... [them] to a merely personal situation."[47] After Jung discusses the symbolic aspects of the famous passages about the seven seals and the Great Whore of Babylon, he returns to the psychological analysis of John.

Viewing the visions of John as John's own violent fantasies, Jung reminds us that these are not in John's conscious awareness. John's letters, assuming that they were written by the same John, speak only of love, whereas the Revelation is filled with deaths of unbelieving women and children. For Jung, John, like Job before him, has seen the "fierce, terrible side of Yahweh," and has learned that "*God can be loved but must be feared.*"[48] Yet, Jung, writing in 1952, after the two World Wars and the proliferation of nuclear weapons, sees much to be afraid of in John's revelation. One act could bring apocalyptic destruction.

> Not nature, but the "genius of mankind," has knotted the hangman's noose with which it can execute itself at any moment. This is simply another *façon de parler* for what John called the "wrath of God."[49]

And this situation forces us to address the problem of evil mentioned above. For contemporary believers "have experienced things so unheard of and so staggering that" the problem of evil has "become a universal religious nightmare."[50] Jung mentions that this problem was also something that occupied Greek and Christian alchemists for centuries. People now have a "new responsibility," and it is one we cannot escape because "the dark God has slipped the atom bomb and chemical weapons" into our grasp, giving us the "power to empty out the apocalyptic vials."[51] For this reason, we "can no longer remain blind and unconscious," we must learn about "God's nature and of metaphysical processes" in order to be able to understand ourselves.[52] After some more discussion of the Assumption of Mary, Jung makes his final point, a point that ties this book to his other works.

> It will now have become clear to the reader that the account I have given of the development of symbolic entities corresponds to a process of differentiation of human consciousness. But since... the archetypes are not mere objects of the mind but are also autonomous factors, i.e., living subjects, the differentiation of consciousness can be understood as the effect of the intervention of transcendentally conditioned dynamisms. In this case it would be the archetypes that accomplish the primary transformation.[53]

Yet, we are forced to deal with both autonomous factors, the unconscious God part (through the Holy Ghost) and the conscious part that asserts our humanity. He closes by saying that

> even the enlightened person remains what he is, and is never more than his own limited ego before the One who dwells within him, whose form has no knowable boundaries, who encompasses him on all sides, fathomless as the abysms of the earth and vast as the sky.[54]

We need, then, to become conscious of the collective through accepting, exploring, and analyzing our dreams and visions. We need to accept the shadow and complete the process of individuation that

Jung has mentioned so often before.

Eastern Religion

Volume 11 of Jung's *Collected Works* bears the title, *Psychology and Religion: West and East*. Contained in the "West" part of this volume are the two works discussed above, as well as some shorter works on religion in therapy and religious symbols, and some forewords to books written by other thinkers. The "East" part of the volume is primarily composed of forewords or introductions to the works of others. Also included are short essays on yoga and meditation. Not everyone agrees, however, whether these ideas should be considered philosophy or religion. This, of course, will depend on how you define these terms. Here, the attributions of Jung and his editors will stand as the issue of these definitions is outside the scope of this work.

In this section, the work to be discussed is a short essay, "The Difference Between Eastern and Western Thinking," which is really part one of Jung's "Psychological Commentary on *The Tibetan Book of the Great Liberation*."[55]   This piece was first written in English in 1939, but was not published until the translation it was meant to accompany was published in 1954. Understanding the ideas in this brief essay will help in understanding the Eastern ideas in the works discussed below in the Alchemy and Mythology sections.

The main difference is that Western philosophy and psychology have come to emphasize the separateness of the individual mind from the community and the universe, whereas Eastern thought stresses interconnectedness. The form that a philosophy takes, for Jung, is dependent on the time and place in which it is created, as well as the personalities of those that create it.[56]   He describes the fundamental difference this way:

> The East bases itself upon psychic reality, that is, upon the psyche as the main and unique condition of existence. It seems as if this... [is] a psychological or temperamental fact rather than a result of philosophical reasoning. It is a typically introverted point of view, contrasted with the equally typical extraverted point of view of the West.... Introversion is, if one may so express it, the "style" of the East, an habitual and collective attitude, just as extraversion is the "style" of the West.[57]

Later he points out that both traditions, though they have their own cultural validation, are one-sided. The West devalues "The One Mind," or interconnectedness, and the East "underrates the world of consciousness."[58]

The differences between cultures, as between individuals cannot easily be bridged. Jung is not sure that it would be advisable even if it could be done. For him, it is better to acknowledge the difference. If we are to get at what is of value in the East (and I suppose other cultures), you must get at it from within, through a process that aims at the same goal, rather than through imitation (or theft). The proper process is the process of individuation.[59]

Alchemy

As with religion, alchemical topics are discussed in most of Jung's mature writings. The works that are almost exclusively about alchemy comprise three volumes of the Collected Works (Volumes 12-14), containing a total of nearly 1700 pages of text.

Jung started becoming concerned with alchemy when his friend Richard Wilhelm presented him with his translation of the ancient Chinese alchemical text, *The Secret of the Golden Flower*. Jung found connections to his own work and produced a commentary to the translation. The translation and commentary were first published together in 1929. For the next twenty-five years, Jung published many papers and lectures on alchemical topics. In 1955, Jung published what he considered to be one of his most important works, *Mysterium Coniunctionis*. It is also his longest.

The reading of Jung's alchemical works is a daunting task, even for those well acquainted with his other writings. He himself says in his "Foreword" to *Mysterium Coniunctionis*, that the material presented in the book "may seem in the highest degree baffling to the academically educated reader."[60] Yet, Jung says this book is connected to other works of the later Jung discussed above (*Answer to Job*) and below (*Synchronicity: An Acausal Connecting Principle*).[61]

For Jung, there are two aspects to the alchemical tradition. He points out in many places in his alchemical writings that both of these aspects occur in all the main alchemical texts. The first aspect is the one that most easily occurs to the modern mind. The alchemist is often described as the proto-chemist, the pre-scientific investigator into the nature of matter. The usual image is the secretive figure in a basement laboratory attempting to turn lead into gold. But this is only half of the story. To, Jung it is the uninteresting half of the story. More importantly, he thinks, the alchemist was a proto-psychologist. On this view, the alchemical work was after the symbolic gold of individuation, rather than the valuable metal. Alchemy was an attempt at bringing up to consciousness the contents of the unconscious, in Jung's view.[62]

What follows is an account of the major themes of these later works. This does not mean, however, that all the contents of Jung's alchemical works are digested below. The reader will have to decide whether or not to attempt these difficult topics.

Alchemical Dream Symbolism

I start here for three reasons. First, aside from the commentary on *The Secret of the Golden Flower*, Jung's lecture on alchemical dream symbolism is his first major work on alchemy. Second, he uses some of the same material in this lecture as he does in *Psychology and Religion* (the Terry Lectures) discussed above, which were delivered two years later. Third, it contains a clear statement of Jung's methodological stance. Some of the discussion of this lecture, "Individual Dream Symbolism in Relation to Alchemy," will be addressed more specifically below when we discuss mandalas, which are not strictly an alchemical topic.

He is using the material in different ways in the two works. In the Terry Lectures, in addition to the general remarks on psychology and religion, he uses one patient's dreams as evidence of his general views that were discussed above. In a footnote, Jung says that although he discussed 74 of the more than 400 dreams already elsewhere that he would be approaching them from a different angle, and points out that since "dreams have many aspects they can be studied from various angles."[63] In the lecture to be addressed here, however, his aim is different:

> The symbols of the process of individuation that appear in dreams are images of an archetypal nature which depict the centralizing process or the production of a new centre of personality.[64]

These dreams have alchemical as well as mandala symbolism. He deals with the more or less alchemical aspects in Chapter 2 and mandala symbolism in Chapter 3. Here, the focus will be on the alchemical aspects.

The method he follows in his analysis is the opposite of what he usually recommends. In this lecture, he does not concern himself with context because of the way in which this large number of dreams "form a coherent series in the course of which the meaning gradually unfolds more or less of its own accord."[65] He also supplies more than 100 reproductions of many kinds of artwork that illustrate the themes from the dreams. In a very clear paragraph, Jung gives us what one might call a summary of one of his most important later ideas:

> consciously the dreamer had no inkling of [his reinscribing of alchemical ideas]. But in his unconscious he is immersed in this sea of historical associations, so that he behaves in his dreams as

65

if he were fully cognizant of these curious excursions into the history of the human mind. He is in fact an unconscious exponent of an autonomous psychic development, just like the medieval alchemist or the classical Neoplatonist. Hence one could say— *cum grano salis*[66] —that history could be constructed just as easily from one's own unconscious as from the actual texts.[67]

Jung wants to make it clear that he did not guide these dreams. In fact, the patient's dream cycle was completed before Jung undertook his analysis of alchemy. All of the themes explained below, except unicorns, occur in this patient's dream cycle.

Mercurius and the Philosopher's Stone

Mercurius is the key figure in alchemical texts. He is also known by his Greek name Hermes, and a whole host of names for similar figures from other traditions like Wotan, for example, from Norse mythology. Mercury is sometimes meant as a reference to the Roman god, but also to the mercury that is the chemical element commonly called quicksilver, that used to be the fluid most often found in thermometers. Mercury is variously allied with the four Greek elements in different texts. Sometimes he is compared to water, sometimes fire, wind, or earth.[68] All in all, Jung considers this "a projection of the unconscious."[69]

Mercurius also appears often as a unity and trinity, a parallel to the way the trinity functions in traditional Christian theology.[70] Jung summarizes at the end of his essay the six main features of Mercurius:

> Mercurius consists of all conceivable opposites. He is thus quite obviously a duality, but is named a unity...

> He is both material and spiritual.

> He is the process by which the lower and material is transformed into the higher and spiritual, and vice versa.

> He is the devil, a redeeming psychopomp, and evasive trickster, and God's reflection in physical nature.

> He is also the reflection of a mystical experience... that coincides with the [alchemical work].

> As such, he represents on the one hand the self and on the other the individuation process and, because of the limitless number of his names, also the collective unconscious.[71]

This struggle to deal with Mercurius, Jung considers an archetypal experience.

The Philosopher's Stone (*lapis philosophorum*) is the substance that would turn lead into gold physically or provide immortality. Jung is much more concerned with the symbolic aspects, which he ties to the individuation process as he does with Mercurius. Like Mercurius, too, it has many names. Each alchemist has a different arcane way of describing it and how to attain it. Jung spends a great deal of time pointing out the parallels between the *lapis* and Christ that occur chronologically in alchemical writings from the Thirteenth through Seventeenth Centuries. The *lapis* becomes a way to refer to the Christ (or God) in matter.[72]

Quaternity

In 1944, Jung published, in book form, the two lectures, "Individual Dream Symbolism in Relation to Alchemy," which was delivered in 1935 and published in 1936, and "Religious Ideas in Alchemy," which was delivered in 1936 and published in 1937. For the book, *Psychology and Alchemy*, he wrote a special introduction: "Introduction to the Religious and Psychological Problems of Alchemy."[73] In this essay, we find a discussion of the importance of the concept of the quaternity. The introduction begins with a reiteration of Jung's attitude toward religion that we have seen in our previous discussion. It is not until more than halfway through the introduction that Jung addresses alchemy specifically. He does this by relating what he calls "the axiom of Maria Prophetissa" which is quoted from a Sixteenth Century alchemical compilation as saying: "one becomes two, two becomes three, and out of the third comes the one as the fourth."[74] He considers this to be a theme that runs through almost all of alchemy. This is the quaternity. It is not just an arrangement of four, but that the One as a fourth member comes out of the third.

He also explains this idea neatly at the beginning of the *Mysterium Coniunctionis*. In fact, in the section entitled, "The Quaternio and the Mediating Role of Mercurius," he ties the quaternity to the topic of our preceding section.[75] The quaternity theme comes in many forms, in many works. Some of these are quite familiar. There are the four seasons and the four elements. Some are not so familiar. Mars and Saturn meet the Moon and Venus (astrologically). There is the four made of the contrasting pairs of masculine/feminine and good/evil. Also there is the combination of cold and moistness with heat and dryness. Another four is upper/lower paired with ascending/descending. Mercurius' role is that of the unifier. As we saw above, Mercurius contains all opposites.

Another quaternity was mentioned above with regard to Jung's

Answer to Job. There we saw, in passing, that Jung interpreted the then new Catholic dogma of the Assumption of Mary as a Christian quaternity that has come out of the trinity. In his lecture, "Religious Ideas in Alchemy," he also mentions the four colors quaternity: black, yellow, white, and red. The four colors refer to different stages of the alchemical process.[76] A final comment about quaternity is that it is related to the *tetraktys* of the ancient Greek Pythagoreans. The *tetraktys* is an arrangement of four rows, which yield ten dots. The way bowling pins are arranged in a bowling alley is a *tetraktys*. The Pythagoreans were Greek philosopher-mathematicians who believed that all of reality could be reduced to numbers and (some) assigned mystical properties to certain numbers. They were also aware of the mathematics of music, harmony, and tuning of musical instruments. The *tetraktys* was special to them because the nice round number ten could be achieved by adding $1 + 2 + 3 + 4$. Plato was greatly influenced by the Pythagoreans.[77] Further quaternities can be found in mandalas, which will be discussed in the sections of this chapter on mythology.

Mysterious Conjunction

The book, *Mysterium Coniunctionis*, is about the unification of opposites that was mentioned above in the discussion of the six aspects of Mercurius. The title literally means mysterious union or conjunction, but it can also be described as alchemical marriage. At the beginning of the book, Jung provides a list of these opposites. As with the quaternities, some of these are obvious and some not. Here is a list of some of the more obvious ones: moist/dry, cold/warm, higher/lower, spirit (or soul)/body, heaven/earth, fire/water, bright/dark, active/passive, gaseous/solid, precious (or costly)/cheap (or common), open (*manifestum*)/hidden (*occultum*), East/West, living/dead.[78] Less obvious pairs include King/Queen, King's son/King's daughter, eagle (that which soars)/toad (that which is tied to the earth), winged bird (or dragon)/wingless bird (or dragon), astrological fishes swimming in opposite directions, stag/unicorn, lion/lioness, wolf/dog.[79] For Jung, these pairs are "transconscious." That is,

> They do not belong to the ego-personality but are supraordinate to it.... The pairs of opposites constitute the phenomenology of the paradoxical *self*, man's totality.[80]

The rest of the book is a discussion in more detail of a number of these conjunctions. Separate chapters, for example, are devoted to the pairs King/Queen and Adam/Eve.

In his brief epilogue at the end of *Mysterium Coniunctionis*, Jung

Religion, Alchemy, and Mythology

reiterates the psychological importance of the conjunctions. Alchemical work, in his view, was primarily about

> the transcendental purpose of producing a *unity*. It was a work of reconciliation between apparently incompatible opposites, which, characteristically, were understood not merely as the natural hostility of the physical elements but at the same time as a moral conflict.[81]

Ultimately, though, this is the same problem that is now faced by the psychologist. What can be done with the opposites that lie at the heart of human existence? Can we bring them to harmony? This is, for Jung how alchemy is an example of the individuation process, though "no single individual ever attains to the richness and scope of the alchemical symbolism," which developed, of course, over centuries.[82]

The Secret of the Golden Flower

In 1929, Jung published a book, *The Secret of the Golden Flower: A Chinese Book of Life*, in collaboration with Richard Wilhelm. This joint publication contains a translation and explanation by Richard Wilhelm of a Chinese text on yoga and alchemy and Jung's commentary.[83] The Chinese text is believed by Wilhelm to have been transmitted orally since around the 9th Century, with printed copies traceable to the 17th and 18th Centuries. It was rediscovered and reprinted in 1920, which is how Wilhelm came across it.[84] He showed it to Jung who found parallels with his own ideas, the ones described in Chapter 3. In fact, Jung's encounter with Wilhelm and the text might be called an instance of synchronicity.[85] Of the text, Jung says that "its content forms a living parallel to what takes place in the psychic development of my patients, none of whom is Chinese."[86]

Although originally published in 1929, the version in Jung's *Collected Works* is the revised edition from 1938. This revised edition makes reference to Jung's two lectures on alchemy from 1935 and 1936, as well as the Terry Lectures from 1937, all of which were discussed above. It also contains Jung's first published references to mandalas; a topic to be explored later this chapter.

One of the first things Jung says in his commentary is that the Chinese text is so strange as "to cause a great deal of head-shaking."[87] Anyone who has read the text before reading any commentary will likely agree. The fact already mentioned, that Jung saw parallels between the Chinese text and his patients, works for Jung as a further proof for the collective unconscious. He uses the Chinese differentiation between yang (light) and yin (dark) as analogous to the relationship between consciousness and the unconscious in an individual. In Taoism, yin and yang flow into each other. Overemphasis of one will lead to a reaction by the other. Since Jung thinks that "modern man" overemphasizes consciousness, this explains the irruption of unconscious, collective elements into the dreams, visions, and fantasies of the modern mind. Sometimes, the balance can be restored by itself, through becoming more involved in something else. He compares this to the Taoist concept of "actionless action," the doing without doing. Other times, the modern individual would have to seek therapy in order to restore the balance.[88]

A dominant symbol in the Chinese text is the circle. The circle is a meditation tool in many cultures. The meditation and prayer circle, or mandala, will be discussed further later in this chapter. Here, Jung is pointing out how the golden flower is depicted as the center of a circle. The golden flower is of the same type as the philosopher's stone discussed above, as it is the key to immortality. The focusing on the golden flower is a way to achieve the balance between yin and yang. For Jung, this process is the process of individuation.[89] This process, he reminds us, includes the integration of those autonomous fragments of the psyche including complexes and the anima (or animus). The conclusion of the process, for Jung, is the self. So, as with the other alchemical texts discussed above, Jung reads this text as primarily a psychological rather than metaphysical guidebook.[90]

Other Alchemical Themes: Unicorns, Trees, and Fishes

There are three other themes that I want to mention briefly. Though not central to his main work, Jung did devote much effort in analyzing the symbolic meaning of trees and unicorns. The third theme, the fish, is more central to his work as it is another way of connecting alchemy and Christianity. He deals with unicorns in the last chapter of the lecture, "Religious Ideas in Alchemy." Trees are discussed at length in the essay, "The Philosophical Tree." The fish makes its appearance in the middle chapters of *Aion*.

The unicorn, as Jung uses the term, occurs in many cultural traditions. Jung allows the word to stand for the theme of one-horned animals in general:

> The unicorn is not a single, clearly defined entity, but a fabulous being with a great many variations: there are, for instance, one-horned horses, asses, fish, dragons, scarabs, etc.[91]

The unicorn is a symbol for Mercurius in alchemy. He further discusses the occurrence of the unicorn in Ecclesiastical Allegory, Gnosticism, Egyptian scarabs, the Hindu Vedas, Persian Zoroastrian texts, the Jewish tradition, and the Chinese tradition.[92]

The tree is another archetypal symbol that frequently works itself into the dreams of the modern mind. Jung starts his essay by reproducing and discussing 31 paintings and other artworks by patients that exhibit tree-symbolism. As with the dreams mentioned above, Jung points out that the images were not prompted by him, and all of them were made before the publication of his works on alchemy.[93] The tree symbol, which has been developing for many centuries, generally represents "growth, life, unfolding of form in a physical and spiritual sense, development, growth from below upwards and from above downwards, the maternal aspect... old age, personality, and finally death and rebirth."[94] From there, he recounts the tree symbolism in numerous texts.[95] He concludes by relating the processes of alchemy once again to psychology, as there is "an apt analogy between the natural growth of the psyche and that of a plant."[96]

The book *Aion*, published in 1951, was already mentioned above in Chapter 3.[97] Although a relatively late work, the first four chapters lay out in a clear manner, Jung's concepts of the Ego, Shadow, Anima/Animus, and the Self. The majority of the book, the next seven chapters, ties together Christianity, Gnosticism, Alchemy, the prophecies of Nostradamus, and the Fish symbol. The last four chapters deal with other symbols of the self in Alchemy and Gnosticism. In these middle chapters of the book, Jung explains the history of the Fish symbol and its identification with Christ.[98] As he says in his "Foreword," he has gravitated to the "symbol of the Fishes, for the Pisces aeon is the synchronistic concomitant of two thousand years of Christian development."[99] What Jung means is that there are several factors that link Christ and the fish. First, there is the matter of the Ancient Greek word for fish, *ichthys*.[100] One reason that is offered for the association is that the word is an anagram for the Greek words that mean "Jesus," "Christ," "God," "Son," and "Savior."[101] Jung rejects this interpretation as being too simple. He thinks the association with the fish predates the anagram. Instead, he thinks that the primary association was astrological. According to ancient astronomer-astrologers, the birth of Christ corresponds to the astrological Age of Pisces, which would last around 2000 years until the Age of Aquarius replaces it. So, as we are entering what many might consider the Age of Aquarius, which many associated with the coming of the antichrist, it is not as difficult to understand why the fish is a symbol of Christianity and why it is now appearing on bumper stickers and as plastic fishes on the backs of cars. Other associations for the early Christians are that the baptismal font was often called the fishpond and Christ was frequently referred to a fisher of men. The fish has the same meanings for the alchemists who were very concerned with astrology.[102]

Mythology and the Paranormal

As with the other two topics discussed above, Jung devoted much work in his later years to themes that we would call mythological or paranormal. We will be concerned here with three related topics, mandalas, synchronicity, and flying saucers. These topics were most fully explored in the last ten years of Jung's life.

Mandala Symbolism

The topic of mandalas comes up in many of Jung's later works beginning with 1929's *Secret of the Golden Flower*. In 1955, he published a three-page article designed to introduce the general Swiss public to the concept of mandalas. His first paragraph provides a good idea of what the concept means:

> The Sanskrit word *mandala* means "circle" in the ordinary sense of the word. In the sphere of religious practices and in psychology it denotes circular images, which are drawn, painted, modelled, or danced. Plastic structures of this kind are to be found, for instance, in Tibetan Buddhism, and as dance figures these circular patterns occur also in Dervish monasteries. As psychological phenomena they appear spontaneously in dreams, in certain states of conflict, and in cases of schizophrenia. Very frequently they contain a quaternity or multiple of four, in the form of a cross, a star, a square, an octagon, etc. In alchemy we encounter this motif in the form of *quadratura circuli*.[103]

In Buddhism, the mandala is used as a device for meditation and concentration. It is usually a very intricate design. Jung thinks that the function of figures in European alchemy that look very much like the Asian mandalas is very similar. These alchemical mandalas serve to unite the four diverse aspects of the quaternities discussed above. In his patients, Jung finds mandala images occurring in children whose parents are divorcing, in schizophrenics whose minds are flooded by the unconscious, and adults who have to come to term with opposites within themselves or their shadows. That is, the mandala brings order to disorder. This ordering effect can account for the therapeutic properties of mandalas.[104] He refers to many places where mandalas with quaternities appear: the biblical books of Daniel, Ezekiel, and Enoch, Plato's *Timaeus*, Egyptian accounts of Horus and his four sons, Goethe's *Faust*, as well as pre-Buddhist Hindu writings.[105] For these reasons, Jung considers the mandala to be archetypal which explains why "despite external differences, we find a fundamental conformity in mandalas regardless of their origin in time or space." [106]

One of Jung's earliest writings on mandalas, a 1933 lecture on mandalas and individuation, shoes how the mandala symbolism was at work in a patient's progress.[107] Using a method similar to the one he used a few years later in the lectures *Psychology and Religion* and "Individual Dream Symbolism in Relation to Alchemy," he analyzes 24 images produced by his patient, Miss X. In his concluding comments, Jung reiterates, as usual, that the patient produced the images without foreknowledge of mandalas or Jung's work on them. He there uses this claim as evidence that the mandala motif is "one of the best examples of the universal operation of an archetype."[108]

In an essay from 1950, "Concerning Mandala Symbolism," Jung adds a list of formal features of mandalas that helps one to visualize them:

Circular, spherical, or egg-shaped formation.

The circle is elaborated into a *flower* (rose, lotus) or a *wheel*.

A centre expressed by a *sun*, *star*, or *cross*, usually with four, eight, or twelve rays.

The circles, spheres, and cruciform figures are often represented in *rotation* (swastika).

The circle is represented by a *snake* coiled about a centre, either ring-shaped (uroboros) or spiral (Orphic egg).

Squaring of the circle, taking the form of a circle in a square or vice versa.

Castle, *city*, and *courtyard* (*temenos*) motifs, quadratic or circular.

Eye (pupil and iris).

Besides the tetradic figures (and multiples of four), there are also triadic and pentadic ones, though these are much rarer.[109]

The rest of this lecture is just commentary that compares mandalas produced in different traditions, including Jung's own productions. Jung acknowledged in *Memories, Dreams, Reflections,* that he included his own mandalas in this earlier work.

Synchronicity

Synchronicity is a term that Jung used in his works on three occasions from 1930-1950 before he prepared a short book on the subject, published in 1952, and a brief lecture given in the previous year while the book was in preparation. In these two later works, Jung provides an extended definition of the concept and a defense of its meaningfulness. The lecture, "On Synchronicity," is the exposition that is much easier to follow.

By synchronicity, Jung means "a meaningful coincidence of two or more events, where something other than the probability of chance is involved."[110] As his first illustrative example, Jung mentions the kind of events that we all become aware of from time to time. Sometimes you will notice in the course of a day a number repeatedly occurring. That is, you see the same number or components of the number mentioned in a conversation, appearing in an address, and on a ticket stub. The individual events are well within the realm of possibility. Jung tells us of one of his own instances from two years prior to the lecture:

> On April 1, 1949, I made a note in the morning of an inscription containing a figure that was half man and half fish. There was fish for lunch. Somebody mentioned the custom of making an "April fish"[111] of someone. In the afternoon, a former patient of mine, whom I had not seen for months, showed me some impressive pictures of fish. In the evening, I was shown a piece of embroidery with sea monsters and fishes in it. The next morning, I saw a former patient, who was visiting me for the first time in ten years. She had dreamed of a large fish the night before. A few months later, when I was using this series for a larger work and had just finished writing it down, I walked over to a lake in front of the house, where I had already been several times that morning. This time a fish a foot long lay on the seawall. Since no one else was present, I have no idea how the fish could have got there.[112]

Since he can provide no causal explanation beyond mere chance, he calls synchronicity an acausal connecting principle. ESP, déjà-vu, clairvoyance, and telepathy are all "mere names" because no causal connections can be established. Synchronicity as a description, though, should be reserved for those "spontaneous, meaningful coincidences of so high a degree of improbability as to appear flatly unbelievable."[113] The example he gives here has to do with an event that occurred during a therapy session with a patient who was difficult because she thought she knew it all. She was telling Jung about a dream she had about a golden scarab, a beetle common in Egyptian art and jewelry. While telling this to Jung, he heard something bouncing off the window. He opened the window and a very scarab-like beetle flew right in. He handed the beetle to her saying, "Here is your scarab." This provided a breakthrough in her therapy.[114]

All synchronistic phenomena can be divided into three categories. The first kind is when there is a correspondence between an inner state and an external event, and there is no proof of a causal relation. The scarab story is an example of this as the dream (inner state) matches up with the beetle flying in the room (external event). A second kind is the "coincidence of a psychic state with a corresponding (more or less simultaneous) external event taking place outside the observer's field of perception, i.e., at a distance, and only verifiable afterward." The example here is when you dream of an event and it is happening at the time you dream it. The third kind is similar to the second, but instead of distance being overcome, it is time. That is, a verifiable view of the future.[115]

From here he talks about two forms of harnessing synchronicity: the *I Ching* and astrology. In the *I Ching*, a Chinese book of oracles, one throws coins or stalks in order to answer questions. Astrology, on the other hand, uses the person's date of birth as it relates to the alignment of objects in the sky as a way of charting that person's life. Jung does not think that the *I Ching* is suitable for scientific testing. Astrology, on the other hand, Jung thinks is "in the process of becoming a science."[116] Using a lot of statistics (that are more fully elaborated in the book, *Synchronicity: An Acausal Connecting Principle*), Jung wished to demonstrate astrological marriages are synchronistic.[117] That is, he wished to show that a certain astrological pairing occurs among actual married couples as a meaningful coincidence.[118] He thinks his data back this up. Scientists do not, in general, accept the kind of evidence he is offering. From all this he concludes that:

> Synchronistic phenomena prove the simultaneous occurrence of meaningful equivalences in heterogeneous, causally unrelated processes.... From this it follows either that the psyche cannot be localized in space, or that space is relative to the psyche.[119]

This conclusion, though, goes far beyond the evidence presented. At places in the longer work, Jung seems to be aware of this.[120] This is important as he strains to tell us in the conclusion of the book-length treatment that "synchronicity is not a philosophical view but an empirical concept which postulates an intellectually necessary principle."[121]

Jung has a chapter on the historical precedents for his concept in *Synchronicity: An Acausal Connecting Principle*. Here he compares his concept of synchronicity with the Chinese concept of *Tao* (The Way). The aspect of Taoism that appeals to Jung is its insistence on the

75

principle of the interconnectedness of all things. Additionally, the yin/yang dichotomy, for Jung, is comparable to the unions of opposites discussed in alchemy.[122] Other precursors are not discussed in as much detail, but he mentions, in chronological order, the Ancient Greek philosopher Theophrastus, Renaissance humanist Pico della Mirandola, the alchemist Agrippa, the astronomer and astrologer Kepler, and the German philosopher Leibniz.[123]

Flying Saucers

In 1958, for one of his very last books, Jung pursued the psychological aspects of the increase in sightings of flying saucers. The English version was published as *Flying Saucers: A Modern Myth of Things Seen in the Skies.*[124]   The book was a response to a misquoting of Jung's view on UFO's. In an interview in 1954, Jung had expressed respectful skepticism about UFO's. He was quoted by other sources in early 1958 as being a "saucer-believer." So, Jung was interested to find out why he would be misquoted in a way to be favorable to saucers. The book then is an answer to the following question: "Why should it be more desirable for saucers to exist than not?"[125]

In the introduction to the book, Jung tells us that as the reality of UFOs is in question, the psychological component of the matter must be as important as the physical. One cannot be sure whether

> a primary perception was followed by a phantasm or whether, conversely, a primary fantasy originating in the unconscious invaded the conscious mind with illusions and visions.... In the first case an objectively real, physical process forms the basis for an accompanying myth; in the second case an archetype creates the corresponding vision. To these causal relationships we must add a third possibility, namely, that of a "synchronistic," i.e., acausal, meaningful coincidence.... It is a hypothesis that has special bearing on phenomena connected with archetypal psychic processes.[126]

Jung cannot address the physical possibilities, but only the psychological ones. Yet, toward the end of the book he declares that even if UFOs are physically real, we still need to address the "psychic projections which are not actually caused, but are only occasioned, by them."[127]

After the introduction, he addresses how the rumors of UFOs spread. From there, however, the structure of the book is similar to his other late-period writings. He has a chapter on the occurrences of UFOs in patients' dreams and a chapter of UFO occurrences in the paintings of patients and others. Next, as with his book on synchronicity, he addresses the historical aspects of the phenomenon. Finally, after a brief chapter on non-psychological aspects, there is an epilogue that contains reflections on a number of topics that didn't fit into the other sections of the book.

Given the ever-increasing popularity of UFO sightings and science-fictional accounts of aliens and spacecraft, what Jung has to say in this book still has much contemporary relevance. Jung traces the (then recent) rumor to the visions of Allied pilots during World War II and the famous Orson Welles radio broadcast of H.G. Wells' *War of the Worlds*. The fact that multiple people have the same visions cannot act as evidence of physical reality. He mentions a number of what he called visionary rumors that have occurred in the past to soldiers during the crusades and World War I as examples. If the visions are psychological projections then "one can hardly suppose… [it is] of no importance whatever."[128] Projections, he reminds us, can be of a personal or collective nature. It is, for Jung, an interesting time to study this phenomenon as UFOs

> have become a *living myth*. We have here a golden opportunity of seeing how a legend is formed, and how in a difficult and dark time for humanity a miraculous tale grows up of an attempted intervention by extra-terrestrial "heavenly" powers—and this at the very time when human fantasy is seriously considering the possibility of space travel…. We at least are conscious of our space-conquering aspirations, but that a corresponding extra-terrestrial tendency exists is a purely mythological conjecture, i.e., a projection.[129]

Remember, of course, that Jung is writing before the first launches with human occupants and more than ten years earlier than the 1969 Moon landing.

As these images are almost universally of flying *saucers*, they immediately call to mind, for Jung, the mandala symbolism discussed above. Of these "round shining objects" appearing in visions "we can hardly avoid interpreting them as archetypal images."[130] Given that we are now living in a highly technological age, it makes sense to Jung, that the archetype would be expressed in the form of a machine, "a technological construction."[131] Ultimately, though, Jung does not think we can draw any conclusions based on the evidence he has been able to collect: "after more than ten years' study… I have not managed to collect a sufficient number of observations from which more reliable conclusions could be drawn."[132]

It is not clear that the last forty years would have changed any of

Jung's conclusions. We can only speculate about what Jung would have thought of the further proliferation of sightings of UFOs and related phenomena in tabloids and other media sources.

Notes

[1] Interestingly enough, he mentions two themes from the seminar, Wotan and Zarathustra on p. 33.

[2] This is what common scholarly usage now calls what used to be called the "Old" Testament. It is called "Hebrew" as this is the language with which it was written. I am consulting throughout the scholarly translation published by the Jewish Publication Society in 1985 and reprinted as Volume 1, *Judaism: The Tanakh*, in the set *Sacred Writings* edited by Jaroslav Pelikan.

[3] The Pseudepigrapha and Apocrypha are books associated with the Hebrew Testament that Judaism has rejected as non-authentic. The Christian bible contains the Apocrypha, usually preceding the Greek Testament, but does not contain the Pseudepigrapha. As the Hebrew Testament designates what used to be called the Old Testament, "Greek Testament" designates what was called the "New Testament." It is called Greek because it was written in the Greek language of the late classical period. For the relevant texts of the Pseudepigrapha, see the Charlesworth volume in the bibliography.

[4] "Psychology and Religion," in *CW*, Volume 11, pp. 6-7.

[5] *Ibid.*, p. 7. See the excerpt from Otto in the bibliography for more on Otto's use of this concept.

[6] This phrase means "religious man."

[7] *Ibid.*, pp. 9-10.

[8] *Ibid.*, p. 15.

[9] *Ibid.*, p. 23.

[10] *Ibid.*, pp. 26-27.

[11] *Ibid.*, 29-31.

[12] *Ibid.*, p. 39. For more on the concept of natural symbols see the books by Douglas and Fiddes listed in the bibliography.

[13] *Ibid.*, p. 50.

[14] This phrase means "natural theology." Natural theology is theology derived from reason and experience. It is usually contrasted with revealed theology, the theology based on revelation.

[15] *Ibid.*, p. 59.

[16] An older term used for a psychiatrist. The novel, *The Alienist*, by Caleb Carr, and its sequel, *The Angel of Darkness*, are turn of the century mysteries featuring a psychologist-sleuth Dr. Laszlo Kreizler, who read Krafft-Ebing and studied with William James at Harvard. The novel contains references to many of the works with which Jung was familiar. Jung himself, of course, would not be familiar to any psychologists in 1896. Jung, it will be recalled, met James on his 1909 visit and became fond of him. James died in 1910.

[17] *Op. Cit.*, p. 64.

[18] *Ibid.*, p. 102.

[19] *Ibid.*, p. 81. Similar ideas can be found in the theological writings of Jung's contemporary, Paul Tillich (1886-1965), who discusses this in terms of "ultimate concern." See, for example, his *Dynamics of Faith*.

[20] *Ibid.*, p. 105. At least that was how the lectures ended. The second edition of the book added another paragraph further urging humility.

[21] The lectures were published as James most popular book, The *Varieties of Religious Experience* in 1902. As was stated earlier, Jung met James on his trip to Massachusetts in 1909.

[22] Jung uses the name "Yahweh" for God. The name "Satan" comes from the Hebrew "ha-satan," which means "adversary." In the Hebrew Testament it does not have the same connotation as it does to the modern mind.

[23] Robert Heinlein's science-fiction novel, *Job: A Comedy of Justice*, is an enjoyable modern variation on Job's story.

[24] "Answer to Job," in *CW*, vol. 11, p. 358. *Assumptio Mariae* is the Catholic dogma announced in 1950 by Pope Pius XII that Mary has been taken into heaven with her body.

[25] *Ibid.*

[26] *Ibid.* See also, p. 363 where he says something similar.

[27] *Ibid.*, p. 360.

[28] Ibid., p. 366.

[29] *Ibid.*, p. 377.

[30] *Ibid.*, pp. 378-379.

[31] *Ibid.*, p. 384.

[32] *Ibid.*, p. 397.

[33] *Ibid.*, pp. 399-402.

[34] *Ibid.*, p. 405.

[35] *Ibid.*, p. 406.

[36] *Ibid.*, pp. 405-408.

[37] *Ibid.*, pp. 408-409, for this and the longer quotation that follows.

[38] *Ibid.*, p. 418.

[39] *Ibid.*, p. 419.

[40] Copies of Enoch were also found among the Qumran documents known as the Dead Sea Scrolls. For a recent scholarly book on the use of Jewish apocalyptic texts in Early Christianity, see the book by VanderKam and Adler in the bibliography.

[41] *Ibid.*, p. 430.

[42] *Ibid.*, p. 434.

[43] The Revelation of John 1:1-2. Translation is the Revised English Bible (1989) as republished in Volume 2, *Christianity: The Apocrypha and the New Testament*, in the set *Sacred Writings* edited by Jaroslav Pelikan. This translation has been consulted for all passages of the Greek Testament.

[44] *Op. Cit.*, pp. 435-436.

[45] *Ibid.*, pp. 436-437.

[46] *Ibid.*, p. 442. A good translation of the phrase *"lumen de lumine"* would be "light of lights."

[47] *Ibid.*, p. 443.

[48] *Ibid.*, p. 450.

[49] *Ibid.*, p. 451. A good translation of the phrase *"façon de parler"* would be "manner of speaking."

[50] *Ibid.*, p. 453.

[51] *Ibid.*, p. 461. Jung makes similar points in parts of *Aion* written at around the same time. See *CW*, vol. 9, part 2, pp. 36, 109.

[52] *Op. Cit.*. p. 461.

[53] *Ibid.*, p. 469.

[54] *Ibid.*, p. 470.

[55] "Psychological Commentary on *The Tibetan Book of the Great Liberation*," in CW, volume 11, pp. 475-508. Part One, "The Difference Between Eastern and Western Thinking," is pp. 475-493. I put "East," "West" and related terms in quotation marks here and above. You should understand the quotation marks throughout, even though I will not use them in what follows. As there are no absolute directions on a globe, East and West are relative to where you are. It would be more accurate to use "Asian" and "European" for "East" and "West," respectively. Jung, though, uses East and West, without quotation marks.

[56] *Ibid.*, pp. 476, 478.

[57] *Ibid.*, p. 481.

[58] *Ibid.*, p. 493.

[59] *Ibid.*, pp. 482-484, 491-492. He says much the same thing about imitating Chinese alchemy in his commentary mentioned below in the Alchemy section.

[60] *CW*, volume 14, p. xvii. *Mysterium Coniunctionis: An Enquiry into the Separation and Synthesis of Psychic Opposites in Alchemy* comprises the entirety of volume 14 of *CW*.

[61] *Ibid.*, p. xv.

[62] For a more traditional view of the history of alchemy, see the "Other Works" section of the Bibliography.

[63] "Psychology and Religion," in *CW*, volume 11, p. 24.

[64] "Individual Dream Symbolism in Relation to Alchemy," in *CW*, volume 12, p. 41.

[65] *Ibid.*, p. 45.

[66] "With a grain of salt."

[67] *Ibid.*, p. 86.

[68] "The Spirit Mercurius," in *CW*, volume 13, pp. 207-220.

[69] *Ibid.*, p. 211.

[70] *Ibid.*, pp. 221-224.

[71] *Ibid.*, p. 237, these are Jung's words. He elaborates on these further in pp. 237-250. A "psychopomp" is a conductor of souls to the place of the dead.

[72] "Religious Ideas in Alchemy," in *CW*, volume 12, pp. 345-431, 475-483. See also "The Visions of Zosimos," in *CW*, volume 13, pp. 57-108 and "Paracelsus as Spiritual Phenomenon," In *CW*, volume 13, pp. 109-189.

[73] The original plan and contents of the book were retained as *CW*, volume 12.

[74] "Introduction to the Religious and Psychological Problems of Alchemy," in *CW*, volume 12, p. 23.

[75] *CW*, volume 14, pp. 6-17. All quotations and references that follow for the rest of this paragraph can be found here.

[76] "Religious Ideas in Alchemy," in *CW*, volume 12, pp. 229-232. Jung points out here, also, that some writers only have three colors, eliminating yellow.

[77] "Individual Dream Symbolism in Relation to Alchemy," in *CW*, volume 12, pp. 148-150, 169.

[78] *Op. Cit.*, p. 3.

[79] *Ibid.*, pp. 4-6.

[80] *Ibid.*, p. 6.

[81] *Ibid.*, p. 554.

[82] *Ibid.*, p. 555.

[83] Jung's commentary, which in the German edition was designated "European Commentary" is published as "Commentary on 'The Secret of the Golden Flower,'" in *CW*, volume 13, pp. 1-56. Wilhelm's translation and explanation were not published in *CW*, but instead as Wilhelm and Jung, *The Secret of the Golden Flower*.

[84] *The Secret of the Golden Flower*, pp. 3-10. For more on the history of Chinese alchemy see chapter 3 of Holmyard's *Alchemy*.

[85] The concept of synchronicity will be explained at the end of this chapter.

[86] "Commentary on 'The Secret of the Golden Flower,'" in *CW*, volume 13, p. 11.

[87] *Ibid.*, p. 7.

[88] *Ibid.*, pp. 11-16. The relation between yin and yang is often represented by the circle which merges white and black, with a white dot in the black side and a black dot in the white side. In this representation, you cannot slice a diameter through the circle to isolate the white and black elements.

[89] *Ibid.*, pp. 21-28. At the end of his commentary, Jung includes ten mandalas created by him and his patients that have a seed or a flower in the center. Also see Wilhelm's explanation in *The Secret of the Golden Flower*, pp. 3-18.

[90] *Ibid.*, pp. 29-43, 44-46, 49-50.

[91] "Religious Ideas in Alchemy," in *CW*, volume 12, pp. 435-436.

[92] *Ibid.*, pp. 439-471.

[93] "The Philosophical Tree," in *CW*, volume 13, pp. 253-254.

[94] *Ibid.*, p. 272.

[95] *Ibid.*, pp. 274-341.

[96] *Ibid.*, p. 349.

[97] *Aion: Researches into the Phenomenology of the Self* was published as *CW*, volume 9, part 2.

[98] *Ibid.*, pp. 72-172.

[99] *Ibid.*, p. ix. The concept of synchronicity is explained below.

[100] ιχθυς

[101] Ιησους, Χριστος, Θεου, Υιος, Σοτηρ

[102] These associations are discussed in threads throughout the later pages of *Aion. Ibid.*, pp. 72-269.

[103] "Mandalas," in *CW*, volume 9, part 1, p. 387. The phrase "*quadratura circuli*" means squared circle. In mandalas, a square within a circle.

[104] Contemporary psychologists sometimes describe the repetitious sayings and drawings of autistic people as resembling a "rage for order."

[105] *Ibid.*, pp. 388-389.

[106] *Ibid.*, pp. 387-388. See also "Concerning Mandala Symbolism," in *CW*, volume 9, part 1, pp. 360-361.

[107] "A Study in the Process of Individuation," in CW, volume 9, part 1, pp. 290-354. This version is a 1950 expansion of the original lecture.

[108] *Ibid.*, p. 353.

[109] *Op. Cit.*, p. 363. These are Jung's words.

[110] "On Synchronicity," in *CW*, volume 8, p. 520.

[111] The tradition of April Fool's Day is an equivalent of this.

[112] *Ibid.*, p. 521.

[113] *Ibid.*, p. 525.

[114] *Ibid.*, pp. 525-526.

[115] *Ibid.*, p. 526.

[116] *Ibid.*, pp. 526-528.

[117] For this exposition see "Synchronicity: An Acausal Connecting Principle," in *CW*, volume 8, pp.454-484.

[118] *Op. Cit.*, pp. 528-530. The pairing is the Sun/Moon conjunction mentioned above in consideration of the *Mysterium Coniunctionis.*

[119] *Ibid.*, p. 531.

[120] *Op. Cit.*, pp. 474-483.

[121] *Ibid.*, p. 512.

[122] *Ibid.*, pp. 485-490.

[123] *Ibid.*, pp. 490-504.

[124] "Flying Saucers: A Modern Myth of Things Seen in the Skies," in *CW*, volume 10, pp. 309-433. The German title, if literally translated, would be *A Modern Myth: Of Things, Seen in the Heavens.* Notice that there is no mention of flying saucers in the German title.

[125] *Ibid.*, p. 310.

[126] *Ibid.*, p. 313.

[127] *Ibid.*, p. 413.

[128] *Ibid.*, p. 319.

[129] *Ibid.*, pp. 322-323.

[130] *Ibid.*, p. 327. The point about mandalas is repeated at p. 387.

[131] *Ibid.*, pp. 328-329.

[132] *Ibid.*, p. 416

Bibliography

The following bibliography is not meant to be a complete survey of work on Jung. Commentary on Jung's thought and exploration of Jungian themes constitutes an enormous amount of scholarship and popular writing. The material listed below is accessible, for the most part, to the average reader. I have included works referred to in the text as well as material not mentioned that I suggest for further reading on particular topics.

Jung's Works

The Collected Works of C.G. Jung, 20 vols. Princeton: Princeton University Press 1954-1976.

Memories, Dreams, Reflections. New York: Vintage Books 1965.

The Portable Jung. Ed. J. Campbell. New York: Penguin Books 1971.

The Basic Writings of C.G. Jung. Ed. V. Staub de Laszlo. New York: Random House 1959.

Man and His Symbols (1964). Ed. C.G. Jung. New York: Dell Books 1968.

Nietzsche's Zarathustra: *Notes of the Seminar Given in 1934-1939 by C.G. Jung*, 2 vols. Ed. James L. Jarrett. Princeton: Princeton University Press, 1988.

Jung's Seminar on Nietzsche's Zarathustra, Abridged ed. Ed. James L. Jarrett. Princeton: Princeton University Press, 1998.

Biographies of Jung

Hannah, B. Jung: His Life and Work—A Biographical Memoir (1976). Boston: Shambhala Publications 1991.

McLynn, F. *Carl Gustav Jung.* New York: St. Martin's Press, 1996.

Noll, R. *The Jung Cult: Origins of a Charismatic Movement.* Princeton: Princeton University Press 1994.

--------. *The Aryan Christ: The Secret Life of Carl Jung*. New York: Random House 1997.

Serrano, M. *Jung & Hesse: A Record of Two Friendships*. New York: Shocken Books 1968.

Subramani, S. Cult Fictions: C.G. Jung and the Founding of *Analytical Psychology*. London: Routledge 1998.

General Introductions to Jung's Thought

Bennet, E.A. *What Jung Really Said*. New York: Shocken Books 1967.

Clarke, J.J. *In Search of Jung: Historical and Philosophical Enquiries*. London: Routledge 1992.

Cox, D. *Modern Psychology: The Teachings of Carl Gustav Jung*. New York: Barnes and Noble 1968.

Fordham, F. *An Introduction to Jung's Psychology*. Baltimore: Penguin Books 1963.

Hall, C.S. and Nordby, V.J. *A Primer of Jungian Psychology*. New York 1973.

Homans, P. *Jung in Context: Modernity and the Making of a Psychology*, 2nd ed. Chicago: The University of Chicago Press 1995.

Hopcke, P.H. *A Guided Tour of the Collected Works of C.G. Jung*, 2nd ed. Boston: Shambhala Publications 1999.

MacIntyre, A. "Jung." *The Encyclopedia of Philosophy*, vol. 4. New York: Macmillan 1967.

Platania, J. *Jung for Beginners*. New York: Writers and Readers Publishing 1997.

Stein, M. *Jung's Map of the Soul: An Introduction*. Chicago: Open Court 1998.

Stevens, A. *On Jung*. London: Routledge 1990.

Storr, A. *C.G. Jung*. New York: Viking Press 1973.

Young-Eisendrath, P. and T. Dawson, eds. *The Cambridge Companion to Jung*. Cambridge: Cambridge University Press 1997.

Works on Specific Topics in Jung

Anthony, M. *The Valkyries: The Women Around Jung*. Longmead: Element 1990.

Dixon, P. *Nietzsche and Jung: Sailing a Deeper Night*. New York: Peter Lang, 1999.

Edinger, E.F. *Ego and Archetype: Individuation and the Religious Function of the Psyche*. New York: Penguin Books 1973.

--------. *The Anatomy of the Psyche: Alchemical Symbolism in*

Psychotherapy. La Salle: Open Court 1985.

Gellert, M. *Modern Mysticism: Jung, Zen, and the Still Good Hand of God.* York Beach: Nicholson-Hays 1994.

Hopcke, R.H. *Persona: Where Sacred Meets Profane.* Boston: Shambhala Publications 1995.

Jacobi, J. *Masks of the Soul.* Grand Rapids: Eerdmans 1976.

Kelly, S. *Individuation and the Absolute: Hegel, Jung and the Path Toward Wholeness.* New York: Paulist Press 1993.

Martin, P.W. *Experiment in Depth: A Study of the Work of Jung, Eliot and Toynbee.* New York: Pantheon Books 1955.

Moacanin, R. *Jung's Psychology and Tibetan Buddhism: Western and Eastern Paths to the Heart.* London: Wisdom Publications 1986.

Palmer, M. *Freud and Jung on Religion.* London: Routledge 1997.

Progoff, I. *Jung's Psychology and its Social Meaning* (1953). Garden City: Anchor Books 1973.

Robertson, R. *Jungian Archetypes: Jung, Gödel, and the History of Archetypes.* York Beach: Nicholas-Hays 1995.

Rosenzweig, S. *Freud, Jung and Hall the King-Maker: The Historic Expedition to America (1909) with G. Stanley Hall as Host and William James as Guest.* St. Louis: Rana House Press 1992.

Sanford, J.A. *Evil: The Shadow Side of Reality.* New York: Crossroad Publishing 1987.

Singer, J. *Boundaries of the Soul: The Practice of Jung's Psychology.* New York: Anchor Books 1973.

--------. *Androgyny: Toward a New Theory of Sexuality.* New York: Anchor Books 1977.

--------. *Seeing Through the Visible World: Jung, Gnosis, and Chaos.* New York: Harper and Row 1990.

Spiegelman, J.M. *The Tree: A Jungian Journey—Tales in Psycho-Mythology,* 2nd ed. Phoenix: Falcon Press 1982.

--------, ed. *Judaism and Jungian Psychology.* Phoenix: New Falcon Publications 1988.

--------, ed. *Catholicism and Jungian Psychology,* 2nd ed. Phoenix: New Falcon Publications 1994.

--------, and M. Miyuki, eds. *Buddhism and Jungian Psychology.* Phoenix: New Falcon Publications 1994.

--------, and A.U. Vasavada, eds. *Hinduism and Jungian Psychology.* Phoenix: New Falcon Publications 1996.

--------, and M. Anderton, eds. *Protestantism and Jungian Psychology.* Phoenix: New Falcon Publications 1996

--------, R.V. Khan, and T. Fernandez, eds. *Sufism, Islam, and Jungian Psychology*. Phoenix: New Falcon Publications 1996.

Stein, M., ed. *Jungian Analysis*. Boston: Shambhala Publications/New Science Library 1984.

Von Franz, M-L. *Alchemy: Introduction to the Symbolism and the Psychology*. Toronto: Inner City Books 1997.

--------. *Alchemical Active Imagination*. Boston: Shambhala Publications 1997.

Wehr, D.S. *Jung & Feminism: Liberating Archetypes*. Boston: Beacon Press 1987.

Other Works

Bilsker, R. "Freud and Schopenhauer: Consciousness, the Unconscious, and the Drive Towards Death," *Idealistic Studies*, 27: 79-90, (1997).

Carr, C. *The Alienist*. New York: Random House 1994.

--------. *The Angel of Darkness*. New York: Random House 1997.

Charlesworth, J.H., ed. *The Old Testament Pseudepigrapha, vol. 1: Apocalyptic Literature and Testaments*. Garden City: Doubleday 1983.

Douglas, M. *Natural Symbols: Explorations in Cosmology*. New York: Vintage Books 1973.

Ellenberger, H. *The Discovery of the Unconscious: The History and Evolution of Dynamic Psychiatry*. New York: Basic Books 1970.

Fiddes, N. *Meat: A Natural Symbol*. London: Routledge 1991.

Freud, S. *Standard Edition of the Complete Psychological Works of Sigmund Freud*, 24 vols. New York: W.W. Norton 1953-1974.

Gay. P. *Freud: A Life for Our Time*. New York: W.W. Norton 1988.

Heinlein, R. *Job: A Comedy of Justice*. New York: Ballantine/Del Rey Books 1984.

Higgins, K. *Nietzsche's Zarathustra*. Philadelphia: Temple University Press 1987.

---------. "Reading Zarathustra." *Reading Nietzsche*. Eds. Robert C. Solomon and Kathleen Higgins. Oxford: Oxford University Press 1988.

Holmyard, E.J. *Alchemy*. Harmondsworth: Penguin Books 1957.

Jaffe, B. *Crucibles: The Story of Chemistry from Ancient Alchemy to Nuclear Fission*. New York: Simon and Schuster 1951.

James, W. *The Varieties of Religious Experience: A Study in Human Nature* (1902). New York: Collier 1961.

Kafka, F. *The Metamorphosis and Other Stories: The Great Short Works of Franz Kafka.* Trans. J. Neugroschel. New York: Scribners 1993.

Kierkegaard, S. *Either/Or* (1843), 2 vols. Trans. H.V. Hong and E. H. Hong. Princeton: Princeton University Press 1987.

--------. *Stages on Life's Way* (1845). Trans. H.V. Hong and E.H. Hong. Princeton: Princeton University Press 1989.

Masani, R. *Zoroastrianism: The Religion of the Good Life* (1938). New York: Macmillan 1968.

Nietzsche, F.W. *Thus Spake Zarathustra* (1883-1885). Trans. Thomas Common (1911). Mineola: Dover Publications 1999.

Pelikan, J., ed. *Sacred Writings*, 6 vols. New York: Book of the Month Club 1992.

Otto, R. "The Idea of the Holy." *Issues in Religion.* Ed. A.M. Frazier. Belmont: Wadsworth 1975.

Robinson, D. N. *An Intellectual History of Psychology.* Madison: University of Wisconsin Press 1986.

Sartre, J-P. *Being and Nothingness: An Essay on Phenomenological Ontology* (1943). Trans. Hazel Barnes. New York: Philosophical Library 1956.

Stillman, J.M. *The Story of Alchemy and Early Chemistry* (1924). New York: Dover Publications 1960.

Tillich, P. *Dynamics of Faith.* New York: Harper 1957.

VanderKam, J.C. and W. Adler, eds. *The Jewish Apocalyptic Heritage in Early Christianity.* Assen: Van Gorcum 1996.

Waite, A. *Alchemists through the Ages.* Blauvelt: Rudolf Steiner Publishing 1970.

Wilhelm, R. *The Secret of The Golden Flower: A Chinese Book of Life*, rev. ed. San Diego: Harcourt Brace Jovanovich 1962.

Yalom, I. *When Nietzsche Wept: A Novel of Obsession.* New York: Basic Books 1992.